YORK NOTES

General Editors: Professor A.N. Jeffares (*University of Stirling*) & Professor Suheil Bushrui (*American University of Beirut*)

Tennessee Williams

THE GLASS MENAGERIE

Notes by Gilbert Debusscher

LICENCIÉ EN PHILOSOPHIE ET LETTRES, DOCTEUR EN PHILOSOPHIE ET LETTRES (UNIVERSITÉ LIBRE DE BRUXELLES)
Professeur, Université Libre de Bruxelles
Docent, Vrije Universiteit, Brussel

LONGMAN
YORK PRESS

Extracts from *The Glass Menagerie* by Tennessee Williams are reprinted
by kind permission of Random House, Inc., New York.
  Copyright 1945 by Tennessee Williams and Edwina D. Williams and
  renewed 1973 by Tennessee Williams.

Extracts from *Four Plays* by Tennessee Williams are reprinted by
kind permission of Secker and Warburg Ltd, London.
  © Copyright 1948 (revised and published version), by Tennessee Williams
  and Edwina D. Williams.

YORK PRESS
Immeuble Esseily, Place Riad Solh, Beirut

ADDISON WESLEY LONGMAN LIMITED
Edinburgh Gate, Harlow,
Essex CM20 2JE, England
Associated companies, branches and representatives
throughout the world

© Librairie du Liban 1982

First published 1982
Thirteenth impression 1998

ISBN 0-582-03965-7

Produced by Addison Wesley Longman Singapore Pte Ltd
Printed in Singapore

Contents

Part 1

Introduction

Tennessee Williams's life and career.

Thomas Lanier Williams—who would later acquire fame and fortune as Tennessee Williams—was born on 26 March 1911, in Columbus, Mississippi, the second child and first son of Cornelius Coffin Williams, a travelling salesman for a shoe company, and Edwina Dakin Williams, the daughter of the local Episcopal minister. The boy grew up in his grandfather's successive rectories in small, rural communities, his mother having decided to live with her own family because of the long professional absences of her husband. In 1919, when Williams was eight years old, his father was promoted to a managerial position which would no longer require him to travel; the family, however, had to settle in St Louis, Missouri.

The move, Williams has repeatedly said, was a tragic one. He and his sister Rose, who was two years older, resented the new Midwestern environment: they felt that their leisurely Southern existence had been undeservedly terminated and that they were unjustly condemned to live in an ugly and hostile environment. At school they were made fun of because of their Southern accents and manners; at home they were terrified by the constant presence of their overpowering father. Tom and Rose became each other's refuge. But then, when the boy was about eleven, his sister attained puberty and the private world they had built together was shattered. So was Rose's mental balance: from now on she drifted further and further away from her brother and from her own sanity. Williams then 'discovered writing as an escape from a world of reality in which [he] felt acutely uncomfortable. It immediately became [his] place of retreat, [his] cave, [his] refuge'.

He graduated from high school in St Louis in June 1929, and entered the University of Missouri in the autumn. He was not a brilliant student, and although he had had a few essays and stories published previously and was awarded small literary prizes in his first two years, as a scholar he was a disappointment. These were the years of the Great Depression, and so his father (who had made up his mind that the boy was a lost cause anyway) forced him after his junior year to take a job as a clerk with his own shoe company at sixty-five dollars a month. Williams has described the next three months as 'a living death'. To escape the stifling routine of a job at which he proved remarkably incompetent, Williams started writing poems and short stories after work, often late into the night. This type of life, which he later recognised as of 'immense value to him as a writer', undermined his health: after a spectacular nervous breakdown which he mistook for serious heart trouble, he was sent to his grandparents in Memphis, Tennessee, to recuperate. During that summer of 1935 he wrote his first play, *Cairo, Shanghai, Bombay!*, a comedy which was successfully produced by a local troupe.

Back in St Louis, Williams entered upon one of his most productive periods: he read feverishly—Arthur Rimbaud (1854-91), Anton Chekhov (1860-1904), Rainer Maria Rilke (1875-1926), Federico Garcia Lorca (1898-1936), and above all the American poet Hart Crane (1899-1932) and the English novelist D.H. Lawrence (1885-1930); and he wrote with inexhaustible energy. At the same time he was enrolled at Washington University, where he was associated with a group of politically-oriented amateur actors called The Mummers, who produced his next two plays *Candles in the Sun* and *Fugitive Kind*; but, again, his academic record was poor. In 1937 Williams transferred to the University of Iowa, from which he graduated a Bachelor of Arts in the spring of 1938.

At home the situation had deteriorated drastically. Rose, who had completely withdrawn from reality, had undergone a prefrontal lobotomy, an extremely delicate brain operation which left her pacified but maimed for life. Cornelius and Edwina, whose marriage had never been a success—in spite of the birth in 1919 of a third child, Walter Dakin—had become completely estranged. At the end of 1938, most of his emotional ties severed, Williams broke away from his St Louis world and headed for New Orleans, Louisiana. He lived there during the winter of 1938-9, sharing lodgings and meals with bohemian and bizarre characters with whom he began to feel a strong sense of kinship.

In the meantime Williams had submitted his early writing to a Group Theatre contest. The judges rewarded him with a substantial cheque and a citation. He also acquired his first agent, Audrey Wood. It was she who secured for him, early in 1940, a Rockefeller fellowship of a thousand dollars which allowed him to enroll in the advanced playwriting seminar of John Gassner and Theresa Helburn at the New School for Social Research in New York. Under their aegis he completed *Battle of Angels*, which was produced by the Theatre Guild in Boston in 1940, only to become a critical disaster. For the next two years he supported himself with various small jobs. In 1943 his agent got him a six-month contract as a script-writer with one of the leading Hollywood film companies. All the projects he submitted were rejected, but the job enabled him to save enough money to see him through the next year. Among the rejects was a scenario entitled *The Gentleman Caller*. It became *The Glass Menagerie*, which opened in Chicago at the end of 1944 and moved to Broadway in March, 1945. It won several prizes and launched Williams's career in the commercial theatre.

The shock of the sudden notoriety, which Williams has described in the essay *The Catastrophe of Success**, forced the playwright into retreat to Mexico, where he completed *You Touched Me!*, an adaptation (written in collaboration with Donald Windham) of a D. H. Lawrence story, and where he did most of the work on *A Streetcar Named Desire*. Based on his experience of New Orleans, *Streetcar* won for Williams a second New York Drama Critics Circle Award and the Pulitzer Prize (1948). Like many of his later stage successes, it was made into a memorable film. From then on, for more than a decade, Williams had a play on Broadway nearly every other year. Some of these plays were hailed, some rejected by the critics, but none met with indifference: *Summer and Smoke* (1948), *The Rose Tattoo* (1951), *Camino Real* (1953), *Cat on a Hot Tin Roof* (1955, the occasion of a third New York Drama Critics Circle Award and a second Pulitzer Prize), *Orpheus Descending* (1957, a remake of *Battle of Angels*), *Suddenly Last Summer* (1958, presented off-Broadway as part of a double bill with an earlier one-act play, *Something Unspoken*), *Sweet Bird of Youth* (1959), and *Period of Adjustment* (1960). During all these years Williams also continued to write one-act plays (*27 Wagons Full of Cotton and Other Plays* in 1946), novellas (*The Roman Spring of Mrs Stone* in 1950), short stories (*One Arm and Other Stories* in 1948; *Hard Candy* in 1954), and poems (*In the Winter of Cities* in 1956). Many of these were preparatory sketches or blueprints for full-length plays; they served literally as Williams's workshop.

The work of the first two decades was deeply rooted in Williams's experience of the American South. Drawing on this store, he had created some of the most memorable characters of contemporary American drama and had enjoyed some of the greatest successes of legitimate theatre. *The Glass Menagerie* ràn for 561 performances, *A Streetcar Named Desire* for 855!

In 1961 *The Night of the Iguana* ran for 316 performances on Broadway; this was to be Williams's last unqualified success. In 1957 the playwright sought to alleviate deep-seated anxieties and frustrations through psychoanalysis, and in subsequent years he experienced a number of personal traumas. As time went on his artistic creativity seemed to diminish and Broadway's interest turned to another kind of playwriting. Williams once declared that he felt as if he had gone through the sixties in a state resembling that of a sleepwalker, numbed by alcohol and drugs. During that period he wrote *The Milktrain Doesn't Stop Here Anymore* (1963); *Slapstick Tragedy* (1966, a double

---

*First published in *The New York Times*, this essay is now included in *The New Classics* edition of the play published by New Directions, New York, 1970.

bill consisting of *The Mutilated* and *The Gnädiges Fräulein*); *The Seven Descents of Myrtle* (1968, alternatively entitled *Kingdom of Earth*, after the short story on which it is based); *In the Bar of a Tokyo Hotel* (1969); and a further collection of short stories entitled *The Knightly Quest* (1966).

With the seventies Williams ventured in new directions with renewed energy. Although none of his later works received a critical acclaim comparable to that which had greeted *The Glass Menagerie* or *A Streetcar Named Desire*, his productivity showed no sign of flagging. During that decade a number of plays were performed and published: *Small Craft Warnings* (1972); *Outcry* (1973, based on the earlier *Two Character Play*); *Vieux Carré* (1979); *A Lovely Sunday for Creve Coeur* (1980). Other plays were staged outside New York but remained unpublished: *This is (An Entertainment)* (1976); *The Red Devil Battery Sign* (1975); *Tiger Tail* (1978); and *Will Mr Merriweather Return from Memphis?* (written in the 1960s but first produced in 1979).

His last original play to be produced on Broadway was *Clothes for a Summer Hotel* which opened in March 1980 but closed immediately because of the unanimously negative critical reception. Three others opened in 1981: *The Notebooks of Trigorin*, produced in Vancouver, Canada; *A House not Meant to Stand*, produced in Chicago; *Something Cloudy, Something Clear* produced off-off-Broadway. None of these attracted favourable reactions from the critics. In the seventies Williams had also returned to the short story with *Eight Mortal Ladies Possessed* (1974), to the novel with *Moise and the World of Reason* (1975), and to poetry with *Androgyne, Mon Amour* (1977), as well as publishing a revelatory autobiography entitled *Memoirs* (1975).

Although the New York critics who first made Williams's reputation became progressively more and more disenchanted with his offerings, the playwright's international reputation continued to grow steadily and his works were translated into all major languages. His literary stature was also firmly established with academic critics and scholars. His position as the most important American playwright of the second half of the twentieth century (the first half undoubtedly belongs to Eugene O'Neill) could be seriously challenged only by his contemporary Arthur Miller or by Edward Albee, almost twenty years his junior. A measure of the reverence accorded Williams by the academic world is the existence, since 1979, of *The Tennessee Williams Newsletter*, a biannual publication, originally edited by Stephen S. Stanton at the University of Michigan and, since 1982, by Jerrold A. Phillips at Northeastern University. The student is referred to this journal for information on recent developments in the criticism concerning the playwright.

Tennessee Williams died in New York, on February 26, 1983.

A note on the text

The text of the play used in the preparation of these Notes is The New Classics edition published by New Directions, New York, 1970. Page references follow quotations from this text. Basically the same text was published by Penguin Books, Harmondsworth, in 1969, in a volume also containing *Sweet Bird of Youth* and *A Streetcar Named Desire*.

The fact is that there exist a number of published versions of *The Glass Menagerie*. Thus students should not be surprised to find a number of minor variants if they use another published version. Alternative texts contain variations in words or phrases but never in speeches or scenes. However, the acting version, that is, the text for theatre professionals published by Dramatists Play Service, New York, 1948, differs from other versions in two important respects: it omits the use of a screen (discussed in Part 3 under 'Set') and introduces two innovations. This text starts with a vituperative speech by Amanda in which she explains her anger at being refused a pew in a nearby Episcopalian church, a change which both introduces Amanda's social pretensions and the contrast between her Southern background and the 'Northern' context of the play. A stage direction in the acting version, moreover, requires Tom to wear his sailor's outfit to deliver the Epilogue as well as (as in other versions) the Prologue, thus stressing the inevitability of the play's outcome.

Other differences between the various versions and the acting version and their influence on the characterisation of Amanda have been studied by James L. Rowland in his article 'Tennessee's Two Amandas', *Research Studies* XXXV, 4, 1967, pp. 331–40.

Part 2

Summaries
of THE GLASS MENAGERIE

MORE THAN ANY OTHER American playwright of his generation, Tennessee Williams believes in the 'magic' of the theatre—in a drama written primarily to be enjoyed in production rather than read in a study or a classroom. His personal views on the overall effect that the play should have in performance are expressed in an unusually large number of stage directions. His extensive and detailed notes contain not only descriptions of the set and of the physical appearances of the characters—a feature to be found in virtually any play—but also specific instructions regarding posture and facial expression, positioning of actors on the stage, and even the colour, size, and texture of properties and costumes. They also concern more technical aspects such as musical accompaniment, sophisticated lighting effects, and the use of unexpected devices such as screens and slide projections.

Williams's scrupulous attention to the details of production does not originate in a devotion to verisimilitude—the playwright is not trying to be realistic or historically accurate—but in his belief that all these components of theatrical 'magic' will help the play to go beyond the banality of surface reality to reveal the deeper truth of the emotions experienced by the characters. The summaries do not, as a rule, take account of the stage directions, although it is impossible, in reference to what is actually seen and heard in performance, to ignore them altogether. They are discussed at length in the critical commentary on the play in Part 3 of these Notes.

A general summary

The Glass Menagerie presents the story, told in retrospect, of a young would-be artist who breaks away from a domineering mother and a shy, introverted sister after failing to find a suitable husband for the girl. It is rooted in the author's own family experience but is not, as his mother pointed out much later in her memoirs, a faithful portrait of it.*

Tom, the narrator-hero of the play, is a poet with a job in a shoe warehouse. He works as a clerk by day, and at night writes poetry in his tiny room or goes to the movies. Tom feels materially responsible for the family because, years earlier, his father deserted it, leaving be-

---

*Williams, Edwina Dakin: *Remember Me to Tom*, as told to Lucy Freeman, Putnam, New York, 1963, pp.142–59.

hind only a blown-up photograph that 'ineluctably' smiles down on the dingy living quarters.

Amanda, the mother, 'a little woman of great but confused vitality', desperately tries to reconcile her dreams of the past—her memories of a genteel South, of gentlemen callers and elegant parties—with the reality of her daily life. Amanda does not let nostalgia interfere with current circumstances, however; she is practical and knows that steps have to be taken to cope with the changed conditions of life. Amanda is much concerned about Tom's increasingly absorbing side activities, which impair his efficiency at work and jeopardise his position at the warehouse. But she is considerably more anxious about Laura, her crippled daughter, who has given up the fight with real life and has retreated into a dream world of little glass animals and scratchy old records. Laura's involvement with the glass figurines is so intense that she has become like 'a piece of her own glass collection, too exquisitely fragile to move from the shelf'.

A first attempt to substitute reality for dreams has misfired. Laura registered for a secretarial course in a business school but dropped out shortly after the beginning of the year because she could not stand confrontation with real people. Deeply upset both by the disappointing outcome of her plan and by the financial loss it represents, Amanda has come to the conclusion that, for Laura, there is only one solution: a suitable husband must be found to provide material and emotional security. It will be Tom's delicate task to select the eligible bachelor and to invite him to dinner.

Tom is unwilling and sceptical at first, but Amanda eventually persuades him to bring home a gentleman caller, a fellow employee at the warehouse, called Jim O'Connor. Jim happens to have been Laura's secret idol in high school, where they took a singing class together, and when the girl learns who the visitor is, she is so upset that she cannot bring herself to come to the table for dinner.

The evening nevertheless proceeds beautifully, with Amanda entertaining the guest in true Southern fashion until the lights go off because Tom has failed to pay the bill, using the money instead to join the seamen's union. Alert to the opportunity, Amanda sends Jim, with a lighted candelabrum, into the living room, where Laura has been lying tensely on the sofa. Jim's simplicity and warmheartedness soon overcome Laura's extreme shyness, and after a few minutes of awkward embarrassment she starts chatting more confidently.

He tells her about his ambitions for the future, his night school courses in public speaking and electrodynamics; she relates her fanciful dreams involving the figurines of her glass collection and dwells in particular on her favourite among the tiny animals, a crystal unicorn. A moment later, while dancing with Laura, Jim inadvertently bumps against the table, and the unicorn falls and breaks its horn. Laura musingly picks it up, commenting that it is now normal like the others.

Inexplicably moved by this strange girl, Jim diagnoses Laura's odd behaviour as the result of an inferiority complex which he imagines he can cure with a kiss. For a brief moment Laura emerges from her dream world. Appalled at the feelings he has awakened in her, Jim clumsily reveals that he is already engaged and is to be married soon. Laura, unable to speak, gently takes Jim's hand and carefully places the broken unicorn in it. Then Amanda, laughing gaily, returns carrying a pitcher of lemonade. When she invites Jim to come back for other visits, he goes through the embarrassing explanation again and then hastily leaves.

Amanda spitefully turns to Tom, reproaching him for his stupidity and his ignorance of reality. Tom stalks off to the movies. Before comforting her daughter, who has now withdrawn for good into her private world, Amanda screams after him that he can 'go to the moon', being nothing but a selfish dreamer.

In the closing scene Tom, as narrator, explains that shortly after the gentleman caller disaster he was fired from the factory and escaped from the house to follow in his roving father's footsteps. While he thus addresses the audience, Amanda is seen in the living room, as though through a sound-proof glass, soothingly talking to Laura. Tom sadly acknowledges that the diversions of the outside world have not erased the memory of his fragile sister. The whole play portrays Tom's unsuccessful attempt to come to terms with a past that haunts him. As the scene dissolves he addresses the candlelit figure of Laura and half-pleadingly, half-commandingly says: 'nowadays the world is lit by lightning! Blow out your candles, Laura—and so good-bye.'

✳Detailed summaries

Scene One

Tom Wingfield enters, dressed as a merchant sailor, and while lighting a cigarette addresses the audience across the footlights. He introduces himself as the narrator of the play and, at the same time, a character in it. He claims that the story he is about to unfold is not a fiction but the truth presented under the pleasant disguise of theatrical illusion. Sketching in the social background of his tale, he invites the audience to return in imagination to the time of the events, the 1930s, when Spain was rent by civil war and the United States witnessed labour disturbances in major cities such as Chicago, Cleveland and St Louis. The play being a recollection, it will be dimly lighted to suggest distance in time; and it will be accompanied by music, because memory sentiment-alises past events.

Tom now introduces the other characters: his mother, Amanda; his sister, Laura; and a gentleman caller, Jim O'Connor, who appears in the last two scenes and who represents a world of reality unknown to the Wingfields. Finally he points to a large photograph over the mantel-piece—a picture of his father, who never appears on the stage but of whom we learn that he held a job with the telephone company until one day he deserted his wife and children to roam the world. The last com-munication the family received from him was a picture postcard from Mexico without an address.

During Tom's first speech, Amanda and Laura are seen through the apartment's transparent fourth wall, which ascends out of sight as the action of the play proper begins (for a discussion of lighting, music, and effects see Part 3, 'The set'). They are seated at a small dining-room table, waiting for Tom to join them for grace before dinner. Once they start eating, Amanda constantly criticises Tom's table manners. She recommends that he should push his food onto his fork with a crust of bread instead of with his fingers, and that he should eat in a leisurely way; unlike animals, which digest without masticating, human beings must chew before swallowing in order to give their salivary glands a chance to function and to appreciate the subtle flavours of a well-cooked meal. Tom is disgusted with his mother's physiological talk and her constant nagging about his behaviour. He leaves the table abruptly to fetch some cigarettes from the kitchen. Laura offers to bring in the dessert but her mother will not let her play the servant; she wants her to look fresh and pretty for possible visitors. When Laura protests that she is not expecting any, Amanda reminisces about the time when she, as a young girl, did not expect gentleman callers either and no less than seventeen appeared on the same Sunday afternoon.

Although Tom and Laura have heard this story many times before, they humour Amanda as she describes at length how she entertained her callers. Amanda recalls the graceful afternoons in the Southern community of Blue Mountain, when girls like her made witty conversa-tion with their gallants. The gentlemen Amanda knew were all rich young planters, many of whom have since died, leaving their widows well provided for. Her recollections come to a sudden halt when she remembers that she had a chance to marry any one of them but chose Mr Wingfield instead. Laura now offers to clear the table but again Amanda refuses, asking her, as she takes in the dishes, how many gentlemen callers will show up. When Laura replies that she is not expecting any, Amanda exclaims from backstage that there must have been a flood or a tornado that is preventing them from calling. Almost to herself Laura explains that she is simply not so popular as her mother once was; to Tom, as if to apologise for Amanda's unrealistic expectations, she says, 'Mother's afraid I'm going to be an old maid'.

NOTES AND GLOSSARY:

It is traditionally at the beginning of a play that the dramatist informs his audience of all that they need to know in order to be able to follow what is to come. This is where he introduces, directly or indirectly, his dramatic material, setting the historical and geographical location of the action, introducing the main characters with their individual personalities and problems, and broaching the nature and possible development of the conflict. The function of these initial moments is known as dramatic exposition. Ideally the exposition should initiate the action, capture the attention of the audience, and awaken their interest in the possible outcome of the play. It should also to some extent establish the tone and style of the performance.

The exposition, then, is the foundation stone on which the rest of the play is based; its importance can hardly be overstated. It represents a difficult task for the playwright, since it requires him to tell in a natural and seemingly unforced way what the characters in the play presumably know already. Playwrights of the past have developed a number of economical and elegant strategies for dealing with this necessity. Williams solves the problem of exposition in part by casting Tom in a double role, as both narrator and character. As narrator, Tom appears among others in the beginning of Scene One to inform us directly of what we ought to know if we are to understand and become interested in the story of the Wingfields.

At first sight the device of the narrator seems to represent an easy solution to the problem of exposition, and the reader might wonder why playwrights have not used it more often. Part of the answer is that such a device draws undue attention to the theatrical, and hence artificial, experience of the audience: if we are to pretend, as indeed playwrights have wanted us to pretend since the advent of realism and naturalism in the nineteenth century, that what we see on the stage is a representation of real life, then a narrator—somebody who stands apart from the dramatic events—is resented as a breach of the convention. In real life we are never confronted with a character who 'stands apart' or 'steps out' to explain or elucidate for us. Such a character disrupts our traditional apprehension of reality and consequently destroys part of the credibility of the play as a picture of life 'as it is'.

At this point the reader should consider for himself what advantages Williams derives from his use of a narrator. How does the playwright integrate this figure into the fabric of the play, glossing over his disruptive nature as a device and making him acceptable? The reader might also come back to the problem of the narrator after reading the

entire play and try to reassess the drawbacks and discern the inconsistencies inherent in the use of this device. These various problems are
discussed in Part 3 under 'Structure'.

The first scene is one of domestic life. It introduces us to the three
members of the Wingfield family at supper. Bearing in mind that this is
the exposition scene, the reader should consider what Williams has
managed to convey about each of the characters individually and about
their relationships. Forgetting for a moment the information imparted
by the narrator, what possible developments could you imagine for the
play after Scene One? Remembering that the narrator in reality introduced five characters, the reader might usefully examine the repeated
allusions to the missing figures of the father and the gentleman caller.
Do we at this point sympathise with one of the characters on stage more
than with the others? If so, with which one, and why? Do the opening
comments of the narrator, viewed in the light of the scene that follows,
provide us with definite clues as to the direction the play is now likely to
take? What direction could that be? Is it likely to capture the attention
of the audience and awaken their interest in the possible outcome of
the play? Why?

The language used in this scene, as indeed throughout the play, is the
standard contemporary American variety of English. Yet to appreciate
William's fine ear for nuances of speech, the reader must remain alert
to differences in language established among the four characters and to
the psychological differences that these imply.

Most obvious is the contrast between Tom and his mother. As a
would-be poet or writer, Tom is aware of language and its possibilities:
his ironic description in Scene Three of the style used in magazines for
matrons establishes his skill at evaluating such contemporary American
attempts at 'literature'. As narrator and character, he is usually given a
straightforward, unaffected, yet highly articulate language that fits his
personality and experience. The occasional swear-word that escapes
him testifies to his impulsive nature and to the pressures under which
he labours. Often, as a character, he waxes lyrical in envisaging the
future and conversely, as a narrator, he grows elegiac in evoking the
past.

In contrast to her 'contemporary' son, Amanda uses words and
phrases that betray her genteel background and provide glimpses of the
Southern belle she once was. Although the attentive reader can pinpoint
these expressions in almost any one of her longer speeches—many will
be elucidated in the comments below—these linguistic remnants of her
former greatness are most evident in the later scene with the gentleman
caller, where she reverts, even in dress, to her identity as a girl in Blue
Mountain. Amanda's speech is further characterised by a use of maxims
or proverbial sayings that reveals her conventional mentality, her ad-

herence to standards, not exclusively linguistic, of the past. The lyricism of her longer speeches also betrays her emotional entanglement in an era which she refuses to consider over.

The various registers and tones traceable in the characters' speeches thus faithfully mirror, in the best tradition of psychological drama, the states of minds or moods of the speakers. The reader should examine any one of the scenes or shorter divisions in the play and try, with the help of the notes and comments provided, to establish the relationship (always carefully maintained by the playwright) between the language and the speaker.

Notice that Laura often remains a silent witness to events and thus provides less opportunity for characterisation through language. One could even argue that her silence or reticence—as opposed to her mother's rhetorical expansiveness and, later, to Jim's obvious 'gift of gab'—provides the main element of contrast between the fragile girl and her interlocutors. For further discussion of this point, see Part 3, 'Characters: Laura'.

A further linguistic element is the particular accent in which the dialogue of the play is spoken. Williams is a Southern writer; his play concerns characters whose roots plunge deep into the culture of the Southern United States. Directors therefore often instruct the actors to imitate the particular local pattern of speech commonly referred to as a 'Southern drawl'. Although it is not essential to an understanding of the play, the reader may form an impression of that regional variety of American English from a reading of *The Glass Menagerie* recorded by Williams himself (*Tennessee Williams: Selections from His Writings*, Caedmon TC 1005, New York, 1952).

The opening scene contains the first of a series of long speeches delivered by various characters practically without interruption by others. These speeches, a characteristic feature of Williams's plays, contain some of his best writing and have often been compared to operatic arias or airs, the bravura moments in which the action proper freezes while the audience is tacitly invited to concentrate on the sheer beauty of the music and virtuosity of a single singer. Williams, however, does not merely indulge himself as a writer in such cases. Amanda's description of her former gentlemen callers, for example, is more than a piece of brilliant writing or a good speech designed to provide a gifted actress with a great moment on the stage. The reader should try to determine what other function is served by this speech; how it contributes to Amanda's psychological portrait and to the picture of her background; and how Tom's reactions to it may broadly hint at the playwright's own attitude toward Amanda and the values she represents. Possible answers to these queries and related matters are provided in Part 3 under 'Characters: Amanda'.

He gives you illusion that has the appearance of truth. I give you truth in the pleasant disguise of illusion: Tom here insists that unlike the stage magician, whose tricks are so well rehearsed that they may have a semblance of truth (compare Scene Four, where the water seems to have turned into wine and the wine in turn into bourbon), he is using stagecraft, that is, an illusionistic presentation, to reveal what is essentially true about the past of his family

The huge middle class of America was matriculating in a school for the blind. Their eyes had failed them, or they had failed their eyes, and so they were having their fingers pressed forcibly down on the fiery Braille alphabet of a dissolving economy: Tom is alluding to the big economic depression that started with the crash of Wall Street on 29 October 1929, provoking the financial ruin of thousands of businesses and a prolonged period of unemployment. The middle class of America had lost any sense of direction, bewildered by the unexpected turn of financial events. They had not been able to see the catastrophe coming or had refused to see what Amanda calls 'the handwriting on the wall'. Hence they had to learn painfully to decipher their new situation, as a blind man reads a raised text printed especially for his use

Guernica: the holy city of the Basque country in the north of Spain. In 1937, during the Spanish Civil War, the city was practically wiped off the map by the bombardments of the Condor legion, the German allies of the Francist troops. The horror of the event, in which almost the entire civilian population was killed, is recorded in Picasso's mural 'Guernica', for a long time on loan to the Museum of Modern Art in New York City and now back in Spain

we can't say grace: we cannot say our usual prayer before the meal

temperament like a Metropolitan star: allusion to the Metropolitan Opera House in New York City, where the most famous, and presumably the most eccentric and high-strung artists perform

I'll be the darky: darky from dark (skinned); that is, a Negro. Amanda is offering to play the servant as blacks did in her youth in the South

the nigger: the black servant. Today the word is an insult

[Tom] plays this scene as though reading from a script: other versions read 'as though he held the book', that is, as if Tom held in his hands the text which he knows Amanda is going to recite

prominent young planters of the Mississippi Delta: owners of large agricultural estates producing the finest cotton in the United States

as though all of my old admirers had turned up their toes to the daisies: as if they had all died and been buried

the Midas touch: Midas was a legendary King of Phrygia whose touch turned everything to gold; figuratively, a businessman who is successful at whatever he undertakes

---

Scene Two

Some time has presumably elapsed since Scene One. When the lights come up, Laura is alone in the apartment washing and polishing her glass collection. As she hears her mother's footsteps, she hurriedly puts the little figurines away and pretends to busy herself with a diagram of a typewriter keyboard. When Amanda comes in it is immediately apparent from her face and weary attitude that she has had an unpleasant experience. Laura greets her nervously but Amanda pretends for the moment not to hear her, and slowly takes off her gloves and hat. When Laura wishes to know about the meeting of the Daughters of the American Revolution that her mother had planned to attend, Amanda curtly retorts that she could not go after all and then moves to the typewriter keyboard diagram, which she tears in two pieces. Staring reproachfully at Laura, Amanda seizes the chart of the Gregg Alphabet and sorrowfully tears it up also, before sinking down on the sofa.

Laura is now very puzzled by her mother's behaviour, so Amanda describes her visit to Rubicam's Business College. She had intended to apologise for her daughter's absence that day, but when she introduced herself as Laura Wingfield's mother she was told that they had no student by that name in the school. On Amanda's insistence they checked the attendance book and discovered that Laura had indeed gone to the school for a few days early in the year but that she had dropped out, definitively they assumed, after a speed test in typing which had made her sick. Laura diffidently gets up and attempts to play the victrola but her mother sternly orders her to stop, and cross-examines her about her actions of the last six weeks. Laura reveals that to spare her mother disappointment, she had preferred to walk in the park in spite of the winter season and her light clothing rather than to admit that she could not face the demands of the business school. She would warm herself at the art museum or in the buildings that housed the tropical flowers and birds at the zoo. Amanda is momentarily shattered by the extent of the disaster. What is to become of Laura? Is she going to sit there for the rest of her life playing with glass toys and worn-out gramophone records? Is she going to become one of those old maids that live off their reluctant relatives, a 'little bird-like woman without a nest'? When Amanda enquires if her daughter has ever liked a boy, it turns out that indeed Laura had secretly admired a Jim O'Connor whom she used to know in high school, and whose picture she has recently contemplated again in the school yearbook.

Amanda is disappointed by the answer, but Laura goes on to tell her that she and Jim O'Connor had a special relationship: once after she had been absent from school with pleurosis he had asked her what had been the cause and, misundertanding the name of the disease, had henceforth nicknamed her 'Blue Roses'. Laura, however, thinks that he must have married the girl to whom he was reported in the yearbook to be engaged. However old and uninteresting the story, it restores Amanda's enterprising spirits, and over Laura's feeble protestations that she is crippled—a word Amanda has banned from the Wingfield vocabulary—the mother promises her daughter that she will get married and compensate for her physical defect by personal charm, a trait she may have inherited from her profligate father.

NOTES AND GLOSSARY:

The first scene concentrated on a brief presentation of the characters and their relationship within the family. Scene Two is devoted largely to a portrait of Laura. It starts in silence, with Laura alone on the stage for a few minutes. Does this seemingly undramatic moment contribute to the characterisation of the girl, or would it be better to dispense with it? Does she appear lonely or unhappy?

Scene Two, another intimate scene, logically prolongs Scene One: we are treated to a 'close-up' of the relationship between Amanda and Laura. What is the mother's attitude towards her daughter? What does her irritation stem from? What do stage directions such as 'a martyred look' or 'a bit of acting', and Amanda's deliberately melodramatic attitude, reveal? What is the girl's reaction to her mother's disappointment?

This scene also broadens our view of the characters. Through the dialogue we are indirectly provided with a glimpse of their reactions not only to each other but to the outside world as well. Keeping this in mind, the reader should look intently at the information presented about the two women and at the contrast thus established between them.

It should not escape attention, either, that Williams carefully proceeds to fill in the background of his tale. What further information are we given in this scene about the South in which Amanda grew up? About the present setting of her life? About the father? About the gentleman caller? The reader might do well to recapitulate the information we have so far gathered about Mr Wingfield and note the source of it in each instance. What is the purpose of having Laura identify by name the character who will later turn out to be the gentleman caller? Does this seem plausible at this point? Later? Why does Amanda show so little interest in Laura's revelation? Do you find the nickname 'Blue Roses' particularly appropriate for Laura? Why (not)?

Scene Two offers a good example of Williams's careful handling of costume and properties for expressive purposes. The reader should analyse in detail the stage directions describing Laura as she is seen in the silent moment at the beginning of the scene, and attempt to relate the dress and properties associated with her to her character and situation. Amanda's entrance should be studied from the same viewpoint; notice the precision of the stage directions about her coat and hat. What visual effect is Williams striving for? What does it reveal about the character and her situation? Amanda is carrying a handbag. Notice its initial description and its subsequent use. Can you discern what the playwright's purpose may be, what point he is making here with this particular property?

Answers to many of the questions raised above are provided in the commentary on subsequent scenes and in Part 3 under 'Characters' and in Part 4.

D.A.R.: Daughters of the American Revolution, a very conservative organisation of women who are lineal descendants of those who were involved in the War for American Independence (1775–83)

Famous and Barr: to this day, the largest department store in St Louis

victrola: a wind-up gramophone

the picture of Jesus' mother in the museum: presumably an allusion to a *pietà*, a representation of the Virgin Mary mourning over the dead body of Christ. The *pietà* is traditionally considered the symbol of extreme human suffering

the yearbook: the annual illustrated album published in American high schools and colleges by the graduating class

The Pirates of Penzance: a comic opera of 1879 by W.S. Gilbert and Arthur Sullivan, often revived in school productions

Scene Three

After the failure of the business college project, Tom tells the audience directly, Amanda's preoccupation with finding a suitable husband for Laura turned into an obsession. To get the extra money needed to redecorate the apartment and buy new clothes for her daughter, Amanda undertook to sell subscriptions to a ladies' magazine. As the lights come up on the apartment, the mother is engaged in a telephone conversation with one of her friends. She first feigns an interest in the lady's health but soon comes to the real object of the call, the renewal of the subscription. After listening to her briefly, the woman pretends to have food in the oven and abruptly hangs up, leaving Amanda baffled at her rudeness. The lights dim.

Before the lights come up again, Tom and Amanda are heard quarrelling. Laura, who is in a spotlight throughout the incident, is crouching in a panic near her glass collection. Amanda, in bathrobe and curlers, must have interrupted Tom's nightly literary endeavours; the typewriter is set up on the table and manuscripts are strewn all over the floor. Tom resents her intrusion, as he resents the lack of privacy in a family of which he is, after all, the only source of financial support. Amanda reproaches him with going to the cinema every night and coming home too late to get a decent rest, thus jeopardising his position at the warehouse. Tom bitterly retorts that he is not in love with his job at Continental Shoemakers and that he envies dead people when he hears his mother's call to 'rise and shine'. If he were the selfish person Amanda suspects him of being, he would long ago have followed in his father's footsteps.

When Amanda accuses Tom of lying about his constant visits to the cinema, he acquiesces: it is not there that he spends his time, he says in a grotesquely ominous manner, but in the underworld of the city, with gangsters, gamblers, and assassins; and one day, he predicts to his petrified mother, his enemies will dynamite the apartment and she will go up on a broomstick over Blue Mountain with seventeen gentlemen callers as the 'ugly—babbling old—*witch*' that she has become. Tom tries to put on an overcoat but his arm catches in the sleeve and, in a rage, he hurls the coat across the room. It strikes the shelf on which Laura's glass collection stands, and several little figurines fall and break. Amanda is stupefied by the insulting comparison with a witch and vows not to speak to Tom again until he apologises. Tom quietens down and slowly goes to his frightened sister to help her to collect the fallen animals, as the lights again dim.

NOTES AND GLOSSARY:

Scene Three is divided into three discernible sections. It is introduced by the narrator's commentary on the business school fiasco, which provides us with an indication that some time has elapsed since Scene Two, and leads us back to Amanda's main preoccupation—indeed, in Tom's words, obsession: the gentleman caller. The play has by now established that this motif always appears in conjunction with that of the absent, profligate father. It is as if the author wants us to see them as correlatives of each other, the two sides of the same coin. The reader should first trace the motif of the father in Scene Three. What ironic message is Williams conveying by constantly juxtaposing these two motifs? Could they be said to have some connection in Amanda's mind? The idea of the gentleman caller also presides over the telephone conversation that comprises the second part of Scene Three and a companion conversation in Scene Four, both of which should be studied in detail.

Amanda's telephone conversation provides an important clue to her character: she shows herself capable of taking practical steps in the world of reality. She seems to have at least an elementary knowledge of sales tactics—from Scene Two we know that she also demonstrated women's underwear in a department store—approaching her subject with a show of human interest. The sales talk, however, fails in the end. Could this be an ominous sign, foreshadowing the outcome of the whole gentleman caller enterprise? Notice in particular the number of details about the magazine—title, style, authors, readership—we are given either through the narrator's presentation or Amanda's sales talk. How do these details help to integrate the telephone episode into the thematic texture of the play, preventing it from becoming merely an extraneous comical interlude? (For further discussion of the telephone conversations see Part 4.)

The narrator's comments and Amanda's telephone conversation form a prelude to the third and most important part of Scene Three, a direct portrait in words and deeds of Tom. During his quarrel with Amanda, we are given more detailed reasons for his feelings and his behaviour. Indeed, we should not lose sight of the fact that the play is also Tom's plea for the audience's understanding, his attempt to explain his seemingly ruthless attitude towards his family. This part of the scene is obviously set late at night. Mother and son are reaching a climax in their strained relationship. What rhetorical devices suggest that these two people are no longer listening to each other? What is Amanda reproaching Tom with? Do you find her reproaches well founded? Do you find Tom's anger justified? How sure are we that Tom's nightly excursions are indeed to the cinema? If they are, can you discern from this particular incident why he would go to the cinema so often? Can you discern what he is looking for in films, what role they play in his existence? Notice that his own long speech at the end of the scene, starting with the word 'Listen!', falls neatly into two parts: in the first he describes his life as a factory worker; in the second, his projection of himself as a gangster. What is the relationship between these two versions of Tom? Is there any reality to his second portrait of himself? What is it that prompts Tom to portray himself as immersed in a life of crime?

Compare this 'aria' of the play with Amanda's earlier speech about gentlemen callers in Scene One, or her later description of herself as a girl 'leading the cotillion' in Scene Six. Pay special attention to the time; the place; the human environment; the moral codes involved; the vocabulary; and the tone of the speeches, to determine their nature and characterising function, the way in which they fit or do not fit those who deliver them. It will not have escaped the reader that they form an obvious and telling contrast, as indeed do the characters. Could it, however, be argued that the speeches serve the same function for their respective authors—that mother and son in fact resort to the same defence mechanism against a world which they refuse to acknowledge because it does not offer them a possibility to be or to develop themselves? For a discussion of these questions the reader should turn to Part 3: 'Characters: Tom's routes of escape'.

Scene Three again provides examples of Williams's use of clothing for expressive purposes. The audience gets a close look at Amanda in curlers and oversize bathrobe—is she therefore being held up to ridicule? Can the fact that the bathrobe is, as Williams says, 'a relic of the faithless Mr Wingfield' be clearly conveyed to an audience? If not, is the visual effect completely lost? Similarly, the incident with Tom's overcoat should be closely scrutinised. In what way can the business with the coat be said to reflect, indeed to summarise, the contents of the scene, and, beyond that, to symbolise Tom's situation in the play and even announce the outcome of his relationship with his family? See Part 3, 'Characters: Tom at home'.

archetype of the universal unconscious: ironic use of the psychoanalytical concepts and vocabulary introduced by Carl Gustav Jung (1875–1961), a Swiss disciple of Sigmund Freud (1856–1939)

Gone with the Wind: a novel by Margaret Mitchell (1900–49) dealing with the history of the South during the Civil War (1861–65). It was published in 1936, received a Pulitzer Prize in 1937, and was made into a record-breaking film in 1939. The book was a phenomenal bestseller; a million and a half copies were sold in the first year

Scarlett O'Hara: the heroine of *Gone with the Wind*

that insane Mr Lawrence: an allusion to D.H. Lawrence (1885–1930), one of the most influential figures in twentieth-century literature. Amanda is probably alluding to one of the better-known novels such as *Sons and Lovers* (1913), *Women in Love* (1920), or *Lady Chatterley's Lover* (1928), the sexual candour of which upset Lawrence's contemporaries but contributed greatly to abolishing taboos

Hogan Gang, The Valley, Killer Wingfield, El Diablo: appellations suggested to Tom by his frequent cinema-going

---

Scene Four

Much later that night—the neighbourhood church bells are heard striking five—Tom comes home. He has obviously drunk too much, and as he tries to insert his key it slips from his fingers into a crack of the fire-escape landing. Laura appears in her nightdress to open the door. When she softly questions him, he says that he has been to the cinema and describes to her the evening's entertainment, particularly a magic show which has impressed him very much because Malvolio, the magician, asked him to come on stage to help him and then gave him souvenirs after the performance. What Tom remembers most vividly is the part of the act in which the magician escaped from a nailed coffin without removing a single nail. That, he feels, is a trick with which his father must have been familiar, and which would come in handy in his present situation. Then he falls drunkenly asleep as the lights dim.

Almost immediately the church bell is heard striking six and Amanda's voice orders Laura to tell her brother to get up. Laura entreats the half-awake Tom to apologise for his insulting words of the previous night and then hurries on an errand. As she steps out on to the fire escape she slips and falls, which brings Tom and Amanda rushing to rescue her. Laura is not seriously hurt, and after an awkward moment of silence Tom apologises for calling his mother a witch and Amanda in turn tells him that her nervousness is due to her apprehension that he might be turning into a drunkard like his father. She insists that he eat some breakfast in order to be able to put in a good day's work, but Tom refuses. In any case, Amanda confides, had he not spoken first she would have broken the silence because she is worried about Laura, whom she had found in tears a few days earlier. The girl feels confusedly that Tom is not happy at home and wants to leave them. Amanda promises that she will not prevent him from joining the merchant navy and satisfying his thirst for adventure in the wide world, provided Laura is financially settled. The only way this can be accomplished, now that the business school venture has failed, is to introduce Laura to eligible young bachelors. Amanda begs Tom to look around at the factory and invite some clean-living fellow worker home to dinner. Tom does not approve of the scheme, but because he is anxious to avoid being late for work he vaguely promises to try. Moments later, Amanda is at her telephone again trying to sell another subscription to her magazine.

NOTES AND GLOSSARY:
Scene Four falls into three distinct parts. The first constitutes the logical outcome of Scene Three: there Tom was seen about to leave for the cinema; here we witness his return. Notice that the playwright explicitly answers our previous question about Tom's filmgoing. The 'perfect shower of movie ticket stubs' that he finds in his pockets while fishing for his key is meant to establish, if we had any doubts, that his evocation of life in the underworld was purely fictional, and that it is indeed in 'cinema halls' that he spends most of his leisure time.

Tom's minute description of the evening's entertainment conveys in part his state of drunkenness: the intoxicated person is unable to focus on essentials, to separate the vital from the trivial, and so he provides us with a complete catalogue of attractions. Several of the details he lists also serve to remind us of the period of the play. The reader should try to discern which details function in this way before turning to the glossary below. Tom himself relates the magic show to his own situation: the reader should review earlier passages in which Tom has spoken of his existence in similar terms. Could Amanda or Laura be said to have a part in this overall picture of Tom's life? For discussion of these points the reader is referred to Part 3, 'Characters: Tom'.

The second part of the scene starts with Laura's exhortation to Tom, which is followed by the small incident of her tripping. Observe how, in word and deed, the girl literally constitutes the link between Tom and Amanda. Freudians would contend that because she is not sure that she has convinced her brother that he should seek reconciliation with Amanda, she achieves her aim by substitute action—that is, by falling, which prompts Amanda and Tom to leap to her rescue and thus brings them together physically if not emotionally.

The scene is significant, too, because it contributes an important feature to Amanda's psychological portrait. If we look at Williams's preliminary description of her in the list of characters at the start of the play, we may wonder at this point what there is 'to admire' or 'to love and pity'—indeed where the 'tenderness' that she is supposed to have is to be found. Thus far her pretence to manners, her superficial optimism, her conventional moralism, her social ambitions may have led us to conceive of her as a shallow woman totally concerned with outward appearances and success. This scene gives poignant proof of her real feelings.

The grandiloquent rhetoric ('I've had to put up a solitary battle all these years. But you're my right-hand bower. Don't fall down, don't fail!'), the proverbial sayings and the forced optimism ('Try and you will *succeed*!') which we have come to recognise as familiar traits of Amanda's psychological portrait are thrown in perspective by her embarrassed, almost girlishly bashful admission, 'There's so many things in my heart that I cannot describe to you. I've never told you but I *loved* your father'.

We are suddenly confronted with Amanda's most intimate self; the ebullience, the nervousness, even the histrionics are gone, to reveal an unsuspected sincerity and depth of feeling. This is a glimpse of the feeling that illuminated her life; at the same time we understand that it is largely as a result of that experience that she has become the unbearable person she is. Notice that Amanda's confession of love for Mr Wingfield comes in the middle of a conversation designed to entice Tom to bring home a gentleman caller. The two motifs are again combined.

The moment of emotional revelation is not allowed to go on, perhaps for fear that it might topple the play into melodrama. The old tension between Tom and Amanda soon builds up again, with the familiar bickering over food, filmgoing, drinking, jeopardising the job. Then the motif of the gentleman caller is reintroduced with a renewed urgency derived from Amanda's inventory of all the attempts that have failed so far. This time she enlists the help of Tom as a last resort. Notice that yet again the incident involves an article of clothing, a muffler. Analyse this fact in the context of the scene and determine its symbolic value.

The third part of the scene is devoted to Amanda's second telephone conversation, which recalls a similar episode in Scene Three. Compare the two conversations and list the ways in which they are alike. Are there significant variations between them? A further piece of information is here given about the magazine. Try to determine why Amanda uses such words as 'strange' and 'interesting' in describing it. For a discussion of the two telephone 'arias', turn to Part 4.

a Garbo picture: Swedish-born Greta Garbo was one of the great stars of Hollywood who successfully managed the transition from silent to sound films. Between 1926, the year of her American debut, and 1939, she appeared in more than twenty films

travelogue: a film on travel

newsreel: a short film about current events

a collection for the Milk Fund: during the Great Depression, it was customary to collect funds at any public gathering to finance free milk or food programmes for schoolchildren or the jobless

Kentucky Straight Bourbon: a whisky distilled from corn mash, originally produced in Bourbon County, Kentucky

Purina: brand name of a breakfast cereal

right-hand bower: also right bower. The jack of trumps in a card game. Amanda emphatically designates Tom as her main support in life

Spartan endurance: Sparta, a city of ancient Greece, was characterised by a frugal way of life, strict self-discipline, and general severity

Jolly Roger: a black flag bearing a white skull and crossbones, used by pirates as their distinctive sign

Young People's League: a generic term used to designate an organisation, sometimes affiliated with a religious group, which promotes social activities among young people

the horsy set on Long Island: a rich and leisurely community—presumably addicted to horse riding—just outside New York City

---

Scene Five

The Wingfields have just finished supper and Tom steps out on to the landing for a smoke while the women remove the dishes from the table. Addressing the audience, Tom describes the dance hall across the alley from the apartment. The young people who gather there are looking for sensual compensation for their dull and senseless existences. But change and adventure, Tom knows, are right around the corner: in Spain civil strife is coming to an end, but in Germany and England the first rumblings of the Second World War can be heard. When Amanda joins him to make a wish on the new moon, Tom half-teasingly tells her that he can guess what she has in mind and announces that he has invited a young man from the factory for supper the next day.

Amanda is overjoyed, but the short notice will not allow her to do much redecorating or looking around for new clothes. When she hears that the young man's name is Jim O'Connor she does not connect him with the school-mate mentioned earlier by Laura. To her the name means that the prospective caller is of Irish descent and therefore presumably a Catholic, which in turn implies that she should prepare fish, the next day being a Friday. But his name also makes Amanda suspect that he might drink, which is the last thing she wants for her daughter's future husband. Tom points out that the boy has not even seen Laura yet, but this does not deter Amanda from questioning him further about O'Connor's position at the warehouse, his salary, and his background. This is how things were done in her day, and by this method girls were prevented from making serious mistakes. Tom wonders how she could then have married Mr Wingfield and Amanda acknowledges that the man's charm had fooled everybody. She hopes, therefore, that without being downright plain, Jim O'Connor is not too good-looking. Tom reassures her: Jim is covered with freckles and does not have too much of a nose. When he adds that Jim takes night courses in radio engineering and public speaking, Amanda decides that he is a young man with visions of advancement in the world. Tom warns his mother that he has not told Jim that he has a sister because, while Laura may be very dear and special to both of them, he knows that the outside world will view her only as a shy, crippled girl who has retreated to a world all her own. Amanda shudders at the word 'crippled', but before she is able to comment, Tom is gone for a night at the cinema.

Full of vitality and optimism again at the prospect of having a gentleman caller, Amanda calls Laura out of the kitchen, where the girl has been drying dishes, and bids her look at the new moon and make a wish. Laura does not know what to wish for and so her mother, 'her voice trembling and her eyes suddenly filling with tears', exclaims, 'Happiness! Good fortune!' as the lights dim.

NOTES AND GLOSSARY:

Scene Five is an after-supper scene at the Wingfields', reminiscent of Scene One. The reader should be aware of the familiar symptoms of tension between Amanda and Tom. Yet, in this scene, we may also sense a different tone: Amanda is less demanding in her solicitude, Tom is gentler in his response. Notice, for example, his reaction to her suggestion that he should stop smoking, or his playful withholding of information that he knows she is eager to hear; or his making gentle fun of her sententiousness. These moments do not, as before, lead to outbursts of anger or resentment. Tom's direct address to the audience also reminds us of Scene One. The speech is designed to recall the wider historical context of the play: the approach of the Second World War.

Tom's description of the ironically named Paradise Dance Hall functions as a reminder of the lower-middle-class background of the protagonists. The dance hall represents an artificial heaven (Paradise!) that provides apartment dwellers of the neighbourhood with a degree of privacy and sensual gratification that is denied them in their teeming hives. It is the place where they experience a temporary release from the burning desperation of their dreary existences; as such it plays for some of them the same role that films play for Tom.

The real business of Scene Five, however, is to provide a preliminary portrait of Jim O'Connor, the living representative of the so-far abstract gentleman caller. The material introduced here is, strictly speaking, expository. Notice, however, that it is presented without awkwardness. Amanda naturally has to be informed of—and thus the audience too provided with—the details of Jim's name and Irish background, his present position and salary at the warehouse, his physique, and his ambitions for the future. Introducing the contrast between Jim's outgoing personality and Laura's timid self, Tom provides a short portrait of his sister as the outside world in the person of Jim might view her. Amanda's protestation—'in what way is she peculiar, may I ask?'—is implicitly rebuffed by the ending of the scene. The reader should put side by side the first silent moments of Scene Two and the vignette that concludes Scene Six to explain why Laura cannot formulate a wish. Does she want to? Is there anything that she really misses? What does it mean that Amanda finally makes the wish for her?

Franco triumphs: the headline refers to the progress of the armed forces of Francisco Franco (1892-1975), who led the Nationalists against the Republicans during the Spanish Civil War (1936-9) and was made Head of State in 1936

Washington U: Washington University, in St Louis, Missouri

Berchtesgaden: an old town in Bavaria (West Germany) where Adolf Hitler had his villa built. From there he conducted his political dealings

Chamberlain's umbrella: Neville Chamberlain, British Prime Minister from 1937 to 1940, thought he had assured 'peace in our time' by adhering to the Munich Pact (1938), through which Britain accepted Hitler's territorial claims on mainland Europe. In public he always appeared with an umbrella, which became his trademark

Garfinkel's Delicatessen: delicatessens are shops, in America often owned or run by Jews, selling ready-to-eat products such as cooked meats, cheeses, or salads

James D. O'Connor. The D is for Delaney: Both surnames establish Jim's Irish origin and therefore his Catholic background. Until recently Catholics made it a rule to abstain from meat on Friday, a form of fasting reminiscent of that of Christ himself. They usually ate fish instead, hence Amanda's 'O'Connor! That, of course, means fish—tomorrow is Friday!'

Durkee's dressing: a well-known brand of ready-made sauce

Scene Six

From the landing of the fire escape, Tom describes Jim O'Connor directly to the audience. In school Jim was Tom's friend, but unlike

Tom he was one of the bright stars there. An excellent sportsman, popular with his mates, intellectually and artistically gifted, Jim seemed bound for early success. Yet six years after graduation he is still holding a job that is only slightly better than Tom's. At the warehouse he is Tom's only friend and indulges the idiosyncrasies of the aspiring poet, whom he good-humouredly nicknames 'Shakespeare'. Tom remembers that Jim and Laura used to know each other, but it is only when Tom asks Jim to dinner that Jim seems to become aware that Tom has relatives. His visit to the Wingfield apartment therefore holds a surprise in store.

The late spring afternoon light reveals Amanda's preparations for the gentleman caller's visit. The apartment has been spruced up and Laura is trying on her new dress. Amanda stuffs two powder puffs into her daughter's bosom, which makes the girl even more ill at ease than does all the fuss surrounding the visit. Amanda herself dons one of the long dresses she used to wear as a Southern debutante. As she demonstrates to Laura how she led the cotillion at the Governor's ball in Jackson, Mississippi, she reminisces about that spring long ago when she had gone from one party to the next in spite of a persistent malarial fever. That was when she had become known as an insatiable gatherer of jonquils; that was also when she fell in love with Mr Wingfield at first sight. This sobering thought brings her back to the present and the imminent arrival of Tom with Mr O'Connor.

Hearing the visitor's name is a shock to Laura. Could this be the Jim O'Connor she had idolised in high school? If so, she tells her mother, she cannot be counted on to come to the table or even to answer the door. But before Amanda disappears to the kitchen to prepare supper, she flatly informs her daughter that she is not going to humour this kind of silliness. Laura is left by herself in the penumbra of the living room, sitting stiffly at the edge of the sofa. After a while Tom and Jim appear on the steps of the fire escape. Tom has forgotten his key and rings the bell. Laura implores her mother to go and let the visitors in herself, but Amanda is adamant and forces the girl to the door. Tom briefly introduces Laura to Jim, but Laura is so moved by the young man's presence that she darts out of the room.

The two men start reading the newspapers, but Jim wants to talk to Tom while they are alone. He advises him to follow his example and take night courses in public speaking so that he will one day be able to escape the drudgery of the warehouse. He also reveals that the foreman, Mr Mendoza, has expressed dissatisfaction with Tom, and that Tom might soon be out of a job. Tom, in turn, reveals to his friend that he is about to leave this kind of existence; he has joined the Union of Merchant Seamen and has paid the month's dues with the money his mother gave him for the light bill. Jim enquires how Tom's mother feels about the project, but it turns out Tom does not intend to tell her: he will follow his father's example. When Amanda appears in her girlish frock, Tom is embarrassed and even Jim is surprised, but Amanda's gay laughter and Jim's warm response soon overcome the initial awkwardness. Amanda chats about the hot weather and the appropriate clothes for the season by way of explaining her incongruous attire. She pretends that Laura is in full charge of supper because she herself was never the domestic type. In the South of her youth, people from her walk of life had plenty of servants; so she never dreamed that some day, having been abandoned by Mr Wingfield, she might have to do the housework. Time has come for supper, and when Tom confirms that the table is set, Amanda insists that Laura join them before they say grace. Laura comes in, but she is obviously unwell and stumbles before she reaches the table. Tom and Amanda rush to her rescue and help her onto the sofa in the living room. Covering up to Jim, Amanda explains that preparing the meal in the hot weather has been too much for Laura. When Tom joins his mother and the gentleman caller at the table, they start to say grace. Outside, the storm that has been gathering all evening finally breaks into rain, as the lights dim.

NOTES AND GLOSSARY:

Scene Six is divided into four parts, each of which is concerned with establishing or reviving a contrast. The direct address by Tom as narrator, with which the scene opens, constitutes a logical link with Scene Five, since it continues the portrait of Jim. We are here indirectly introduced to Jim as he appeared six years earlier, when Tom and Laura used to know him in high school. The sharp contrast between the high-school hero of the past and the factory worker of the present is clearly demonstrated by juxtaposing two sentences in Tom's presentation: 'you would logically expect him to arrive at nothing short of the White House by the time he was thirty'; yet 'six years after he left high school he was holding a job that wasn't much better than mine'. The past, then, emerges from these comments as a period of potential greatness, of promise; the present is a time of disillusion and drabness. This impression is reinforced by the description of Tom's relationship with the other workers at the warehouse, where he is presented as a poet living in complete alienation from the human environment in which he works.

The second part of the scene develops the contrast between Amanda and Laura succinctly expressed by Laura at the end of Scene One—and further established in Scene Two. When the lights come up on the scene, Amanda has literally been shaping a new Laura. In the stage directions the playwright clearly describes the effect of the mother's efforts on the girl's outward appearance. Do these comments already contain hints of the unsuccessful outcome of the whole enterprise? What is Amanda actually doing to Laura psychologically? What is the model after which she is trying to fashion the girl?

Notice Amanda's active role in the scene ('Amanda has worked like a Turk'), and Laura's complete passivity ('Laura stands in the middle with lifted arms'). Consider Amanda's words to Laura: 'You couldn't be satisfied with just sitting home.' What do they reveal about Amanda's knowledge of her daughter? What is the mother implicitly holding up as an ideal to her daughter?

The scene provides an excellent example of Williams's use of properties and costumes for expressive purposes. The reader should determine in what way, by themselves and through comparison, the dresses of Laura and Amanda are expressive of what the two women are or were. Special attention should be devoted to colour and style in this respect.

Amanda's 'aria' about the South should be re-read alongside similar speeches about gentlemen callers (Scene One, pp.26-7), old maid relatives (Scene Two, p.34), enquiries about prospective husbands (Scene Five, pp.63-4), and her own marriage (Scene Six, p.82), to get a full picture of the Southern background as reconstructed by Amanda. Are there, running through all these speeches, discrepancies or sobering touches by which Amanda unconsciously negates or undercuts the great value she attaches to that past? Are there signs that the South she presents to us was no longer or perhaps had never been the idyllic South that she would now like it to be?

This section ends with a rather violent confrontation between Amanda and Laura, brought on by Laura's realisation that the gentleman caller might be the Jim O'Connor of high-school days. Laura's protest that she will be unable to come to the table or even open the front door if the visitor is Jim O'Connor is comparable in impact to Amanda's revelation in Scene Five that she loved Mr Wingfield. Lest we begin to feel that Laura is so timid and shy that she is utterly incapable of feeling anything, we are provided with a confirmation of what we had vaguely suspected: Jim had been much more than a mere high-school friend in her mind. Notice that in spite of the contrast between the characters and experiences of the two women, they are nevertheless comparable on the basis of this 'illumination of love'.

The confrontation also brings back into focus Amanda's realism: after her dreamy flight into the Southern past of her youth, she is promptly reintroduced as a level-headed woman who knows or suddenly remembers what the whole gentleman caller scheme is about. The third part of the scene, besides containing the brief introduction which reveals the extent of Laura's pathological shyness, is really concerned with establishing the contrast between Tom and Jim. The reader should look closely at the brief dialogue about the newspaper, the *Post Dis-*

patch. Why should Tom assume that Jim wants to see the comics? Why should Jim's answer be an exclamation followed by a kind of justification? What kind of reaction does Jim's information draw from Tom? Why? After this brief 'overture', the playwright goes on to delineate the gulf that separates the two men. The reader should be attentive to the portraits of Tom and Jim that emerge from their conversation, and try to determine how Williams works here through contrasting characterisation.

Finally, in the last section of this scene, Amanda's portrait is completed with a direct revelation of what she was in the past—a Southern belle. The reader or spectator has already contemplated Amanda in her 'jonquil dress' but through Tom's and Jim's shocked reactions to the 'resurrected' garment we are made aware of the incongruity between her appearance and her surroundings. The balls and cotillions are shrilly contrasted with the meagre supper party; the Governor's mansion in Jackson with the dingy apartment in St Louis; the rich young planters with the impecunious warehouse employees.

The dialogue—or more accurately, monologue—which Amanda conducts confirming Tom's earlier sarcastic remark, 'I bet you could talk' (Scene One, p.25) gives proof that she indeed 'understood the art of conversation'. But the measure of irony introduced by the playwright is made clear when 'Southern talk' defined by Amanda as about 'things of importance going on in the world! Never anything coarse or common or vulgar', turns out to be typical chatter about the weather, food, clothes, and children. Her speech puts the finishing touch to our picture of a South which she herself says is 'gone, gone, gone'. But as important as the matter of her speech is the manner in which it is delivered. The girlish Southern vivacity called for in the stage direction, the constant, inconsequential chatter, the retrieval of the Southern drawl, contribute decisively to the picture of Amanda as a carefree Southern girl. Notice that once again the gentlemen callers and her husband are mentioned almost side by side.

The reader should also be aware of the irony of the overall situation: a gentleman caller has been brought to the house for Laura and ends up being entertained by Amanda. Does this suggest an answer to the questions asked earlier about the relationship between Laura and Amanda? How do visual elements at the end of Scene Six and the beginning of Scene Seven emphasise this painfully ironical situation? For a discussion of these questions see Part 3, 'Characters: Amanda'.

cakewalk:	a typical American entertainment of the period, in which a cake was the prize for the most accomplished steps and figures in walking
Dardanella:	a popular melody of the twenties

Ole Dizzy Dean:	a famous American baseball player of the period
Gable:	Clark Gable (1901–60), a very popular American film actor often called 'The King'. His most famous role was as Rhett Butler, opposite Vivien Leigh's Scarlett O'Hara, in *Gone with the Wind*
South Sea Islands:	typical setting of escapist films of the 1930s
angel-food cake:	a sponge cake made of flour, sugar, and egg-whites

Scene Seven

Dinner is almost finished and Laura is still lying on the sofa in the living-room. Suddenly both rooms are plunged in darkness. Amanda immediately lights the candles that decorate the dinner table and asks Jim if he can tell a burnt-out fuse. Upon examination it appears that the fuses are all right but that the company has discontinued the service because the bill has remained unpaid. Amanda scolds Tom and forces him to help her in the kitchen as penance for his negligence; at the same time she gently persuades Jim to go and keep Laura company. As he enters the living room with an old candelabrum, Laura sits up nervously, but after a while she relaxes, overcome by his warmheartedness. Jim sits down on the floor next to the source of light and invites Laura to join him; he offers her chewing-gum and muses on the fortune made by its inventor.

When Jim starts talking about her shyness, Laura hastily turns the conversation back to him, enquiring if he has kept up his singing. Jim's memories of high school now all come back to him: he remembers having met Laura when they took singing-class together, and Laura reminds him also of the reason for her nickname of Blue Roses. She shyly confides that her physical defect and the brace, and the noise she thought it made, were so many obstacles to her making friends, but Jim does not seem to remember any noise. She should not have been so bashful; people are not so dreadful and all have problems of some kind or another, including himself. When he mentions the school's yearbook Laura takes it down from her shelves and they leaf through it together, reminiscing about Jim's beautiful performance as the baritone lead in *The Pirates of Penzance.*

Laura never dared to approach him in those days to get him to sign her programme, so Jim now takes the book from her hands and, although he is aware that his signature is not yet worth much and is maybe even less valuable now than six years ago, he signs the programme with a flourish. Laura wants to know what happened to Emily Meisenbach, the girl that Jim was to marry according to the yearbook, but Jim assures her that their 'engagement' was never more than wishful thinking on Emily's part. When he tries to find out what Laura has been up to all these years, she murmurs something about a business course that turned out badly, and the care she takes of her glass collection.

Jim abruptly diagnoses her as suffering from an inferiority complex. Although he is not a doctor, he says, he is something of a psychologist: what Laura should do to overcome her sense of unworthiness is think of herself as in some way superior. Taking himself as an example, Jim describes his interest in electrodynamics and public speaking. He is obviously preparing for a career in television. He wants to be ready when the industry itself gets under way. When he expresses interest in Laura's collection she hands him the little unicorn, confessing that it is her favourite among all the glass animals.

But Jim's interest in the figurines is short-lived: he puts the little horse with a horn on a side table and opens the door on to the fire escape for fresh air. Music pours in from the Paradise Dance Hall and Jim playfully invites Laura for a waltz. The girl is reticent and moves awkwardly at first but lets herself be swept along by Jim; as they dance around the narrow room she relaxes and laughs. When they knock against the small table, the unicorn falls, breaking off its little horn. Jim is very sorry but Laura seems to view the incident in a different light: now the unicorn will feel more at home with the 'normal' horses. Jim is strangely moved by Laura; he feels that she is different from the girls he has known so far and that all she needs is somebody to build up her confidence and make her proud of herself. In a spontaneous gesture he kisses her on the lips, unleashing in Laura a store of long-repressed, hidden feelings.

He immediately regrets the kiss, explaining that he will not be able to come back. He has been going steady with Betty, a girl of Irish Catholic background whom he met on a boat trip the summer before and whom he is to marry in a month or two. Betty is out of town visiting a sick relative; that is why Jim accepted Tom's invitation for dinner. Laura is visibly shattered by the revelation and cannot utter a word, but she picks up the broken unicorn and gently places it in Jim's hand as Amanda comes in, cheerfully announcing that she has made some lemonade for the young people and expressing the hope that Jim will henceforth be a regular visitor to the apartment. Jim, however, declines the kind offer, repeating the admission about Betty. Amanda mechanically wishes him luck and happiness and success before he leaves with his little, broken souvenir, to pick up his fiancée at the bus depot.

As soon as Jim has disappeared, Amanda calls Tom into the living-room. What is this joke he has perpetrated on them? All the expense, the preparation, was to entertain a man who is already engaged. Amanda accuses him of never knowing anything, of neglecting his deserted mother and crippled sister because the only thing he is really interested in is himself. Tom smashes the glass he is holding and storms off to the cinema. As he reaches the fire escape, he grips the rail in desperation. Then, addressing the audience for the last time, he tells them that he lost his job shortly after the gentleman caller disaster and left mother and sister for good in an attempt to forget them and their situation. But his intensive travels with the merchant navy have been of no avail in obliterating his sense of guilt. Whenever he passes in front of a shop window with tiny transparent bottles of coloured glass, he is reminded of the fragile beauty of his sister and her menagerie. Throughout Tom's final speech Amanda is seen in silent pantomime making a comforting speech to Laura. Her words bring a smile to Laura's face, which is illumined by the flickering light of the candles brought in earlier by Jim. As he reaches his conclusion, Tom beseeches Laura to blow out her candles. When she does so, the scene dissolves.

NOTES AND GLOSSARY:
Scene Seven is devoted almost entirely to the interview between Jim and Laura, which is framed by two smaller sections: the incident of the failure of the lights, and Tom's final words as narrator. These two sections should be looked at carefully. The brief, seemingly trivial incident with the lights is used by Williams to add a symbolic dimension to the whole scene and to bring a further meaning to the characters and the play in general. The reader should be aware of the accumulation of references to light; both the beginning and the end of Scene Seven are explicitly concerned with this motif. In this connection the reader should remember that in the Western tradition light is an attribute of divinity; he should also keep in mind that Williams's background is a devoutly religious one, his grandfather having been an Episcopal minister. This aspect of Scene Seven and its ramifications in the play are discussed in Part 3 under 'Characters: Jim O'Connor' and 'Religious symbolism'.

The brief incident with the lights also provides the playwright with an opportunity for a final recapitulation of the attributes of the various characters. The reader should trace in this episode the salient points of each characterisation: Amanda's Southern vivacity, her entertaining character, her past-oriented personality, her sententiousness; Jim's good-natured character, his apparent self-assuredness and social poise. In addition, we see reiterated Tom's strained relationship with his mother and her poor opinion of him as a practical man.

The central part of Scene Seven allows the direct development of several aspects of Jim's personality. (He has already been introduced indirectly in Tom's report to Amanda in Scene Five and in the narrator's portrait of him in Scene Six.) Here he appears successively—as the reader should have no difficulty recognising through his actions or the dialogue—as a former high-school hero (when reflecting on the past);

an apprentice psychologist (in his relationship with Laura); and an average American boy (when describing the present). Observe in each case how the language and the thoughts help to shape these aspects of Jim's character. All of these considerations are discussed in detail in Part 3 under 'Characters: Jim O'Connor'.

In his short-lived but intense relationship with Laura, Jim passes from a parlour psychiatrist who naively thinks that a kiss can solve a deep psychological problem, to an embarrassed visitor who takes with him as a souvenir the broken unicorn. The function of the glass menagerie, and in particular of its unicorn as a symbol for Laura, appears in this scene with particular vividness. The reader should try to discern what points of comparison Williams establishes between Laura and the little glass animal. Her reactions to it should be contrasted with Jim's. For a full discussion of this point, turn to Part 3, 'Jim, Laura, and the unicorn'. For an explanation of the symbolic meanings of Jim O'Connor and the unicorn in this scene, see Part 3, 'Religious symbolism'.

In the brief interval between Jim's departure and Tom's final speech, we witness the last explosion of resentment between Amanda and her son. Laura is once again completely silent. Amanda's main reproach to Tom is that he 'lives in a dream'. Do you detect irony in this final reproach? Do you concur with Amanda's verdict that Tom is 'selfish', that he does not 'let anything interfere with [his] selfish pleasure'? When formulating your answer take into account two elements: first, the playwright's early remark that Tom's nature 'is not remorseless, but to escape from a trap, he has to act without pity'; secondly, the tone of Tom's last speech and the feeling that pervades it. Upon your answer will depend your final judgment of Tom's character and your feeling about whether the play has justified his final break with his family.

Tom's concluding speech warrants close attention. It is not entirely clear whether the Second World War, whose approach was announced early in the play, is now over, but the sailor's outfit in which Tom delivers both Prologue and Epilogue clearly indicates that he has left the apartment and St Louis for good. What is the effect of exhibiting these sailor's clothes at the very beginning of the play? What kind of world has Tom sought to escape and what kind of existence has he escaped into? The very last section of the play is described in the stage direction '[Laura] blows the candles out.' What is the effect of this final moment? For discussion of these questions turn to Part 3, 'Characters'.

Moses:	the Old Testament leader who brought the Hebrews from Egypt to Moab (now in Jordan), within sight of the Promised Land. Notice, however, that the answer, and hence the comic effect of the riddle, emphasises the literal situation rather than the identity of the person involved

Benjamin Franklin: an American statesman, author, and scientist (1706-90) known for his practical inventions, which include the Franklin stove, bifocal reading glasses, the writing chair, and the lightning rod. Flying a kite during a storm, Franklin was able to show that lightning was indeed a form of electricity

Mr Edison: Thomas Alva Edison (1847-1931) was one of the most prolific American inventors. Besides improving many of the devices of others, he invented the gramophone and manufactured the first incandescent lamp

dandelion wine: a slightly alcoholic beverage made from the flower of the dandelion

The Wrigley Building: one of the striking architectural features of Chicago, named after William Wrigley Jr, the inventor of chewing gum

Oh, that Kraut-head!: a pejorative epithet applied to Americans of German origin

La Golondrina: Spanish for 'swallow'. The song, a favourite of the period, is a nostalgic celebration of things that fade with summer

stumblejohn: a blunderer. The word is now obsolete

that was way off the beam: that was a big mistake, or absolutely uncalled for

it's only the shank of the evening: the beginning of the evening

jalopy: an old, rattling car

I'll be jiggered: I'm surprised; that's news to me

Part 3

Commentary

The Glass Menagerie as biography

The Glass Menagerie has been described as 'the most consciously biographical of all Williams's dramas'. It represents the author's effort to come to terms with his past and to transcend or exorcise it. As a 'memory play', it chronicles the story of Williams's last years in St Louis. Much of the information about Williams's early years presented in Part 1 can be traced in the play.* The playwright's childhood relationship with his sister Rose provided the basis for the emotional ties that bind Tom and Laura. Although the girl's name has been changed, the nickname 'Blue Roses' recalls the real-life character. Further, the glass animals that provide the title of the play and a good measure of its symbolism were among the Williams children's toys. The playwright has described them: 'those little glass animals came to represent in my memory all the softest emotions that belong to the recollection of things past. They stood for all the small and tender things that relieve the austere pattern of life and make it endurable to the sensitive.'

In real life, too, Rose took a course in secretarial school but ended up in the park, the museum, and the zoo instead of the classroom. In the play Laura has a physical defect; she is 'crippled'. In actuality the situation was infinitely more painful: at puberty Rose had started to show signs of psychological disturbance which deteriorated into a pathological withdrawal from reality so severe that she had to have a brain operation. This circumstance is poignantly echoed in Laura's gentle reaction to the breaking of the unicorn: 'I'll just imagine he had an operation. The horn was removed to make him feel less—freakish!' (p.104). Amanda Wingfield is modelled after Tennessee Williams's own mother; Edwina Dakin Williams, who died in June, 1980, was equally obsessed with the greatness of her past in contrast to the shabbiness of her life in St Louis. She also belonged to the D.A.R., of which she was a regent, and insisted on maintaining genteel manners and behaviour at home. In real life, as in the play, she enlisted Tom to bring home suitable gentlemen callers. Such visits as there were invariably turned into embarrassments for Tom and his sister when their mother overwhelmed everybody with her vivacious 'Southern' conversation.

*For many more details taken from real life, the reader should consult the sources of biographical information listed in the bibliography.

The father, whom Williams hated so much that he could not dramatise him except in the gallantly smiling photograph over the mantle, had
not actually left the family for a free-roaming existence. But as a travelling salesman he had often been away on business, and even after the
move to St Louis, when he became a manager in the company, he doled
out money reluctantly—although his salary was good—and kept the
family in a state of near-poverty.

Tom is also in part a portrait of Williams. Their Christian names are
the same and although the fictional surname of the character in the play
differs from that of the author, their initials—T.W.—are identical. Both
are enthusiastic admirers of D.H. Lawrence and compulsive smokers,
drinkers, and filmgoers. Williams presents Tom as 'a poet with a job
in a warehouse': the playwright, too, had been forced to take a job in a
local shoe company. The firm's name is ironically altered in the play
from 'International Shoe Company' to 'Continental Shoemakers', but
the monthly salary—the low amount of sixty-five dollars—is the same
as that earned by the young clerk Williams. In real life, too, Williams
used to retire to the lavatory to work on poems. More significant than
the details of the job and its financial implications, the feelings aroused
in Williams by the situation also found their way into the play. The
confinement of the young poet in the office compounded with the dis-
tress of his home life dominate Tom's entire existence and become his
main incentives to action.

Finally, even the drabness of the setting has its roots in Williams's
biography, reflecting Williams's horrified reaction to the St Louis
environment into which he and his sister had unwillingly been thrust at
an early age. But not all the material of the play is autobiographical;
the picture is not a strictly accurate one. Williams selected among, com-
pressed, and otherwise modified the raw materials of his immediate
experience. In the process, *The Glass Menagerie* ceased to be a personal
record of endured hardship and became a compelling fable for the
stage. It acquired the exemplary meaning and dignity that belongs only
to art, snatching as it does, 'the eternal out of the desperately fleeting'.*

Structure and narrative device

The Glass Menagerie is described by Williams as a 'static' play (p.10),
by which he means a drama that has little organic movement other than
that of its chronological development. Indeed the play is, in effect, a
picture of a situation; the interest depends neither on incident nor
action. Williams also says that the play is 'episodic'—that is, it is a play
in which the various elements of action are perceived and presented as
units distinct and separate from each other rather than forming a con-

*In 'The Timeless World of a Play', introduction to *The Rose Tattoo* (1951).

tinuum or composing a unity. The division of the play into seven scenes of varying length (themselves sometimes subdivided into further scenic units) strongly emphasises the static and episodic nature of the play. The summaries and accompanying comments presented here have attempted to give some notion of this. But Williams has made use of a number of theatrical devices to overcome a damaging impression of fragmentation or stasis: the flexible set, the musical leitmotif, and imaginative lighting effects (see 'The set'). Even more effective than these devices, however, is the use of a narrator. In the play, Tom Wingfield appears in a double capacity, as both narrator of the play and a character in it. Williams carefully establishes the difference between the two functions. As narrator, Tom always addresses the audience directly. In so doing he acknowledges his awareness of its presence across the footlights, presents himself as the contemporary of his listeners and thus provides a historical perspective for the tale he unfolds. As narrator Tom is sometimes costumed differently from Tom the character: in the first and last scenes, he appears dressed as a merchant sailor. In Scenes Three to Six, Tom the narrator speaks from a particular place on the stage. The landing of the fire escape becomes a sort of witness stand from which, part witness and part accused, he delivers his speeches.

The narrator fulfils at least two clear functions; he is a convenient means of exposition, both supplying information and setting the tone and style of the production; and he provides easy continuity between events otherwise disconnected in time. Although the two functions are not consistently distinct, it is easy to determine that Tom is essentially narrator-expositor in Scenes One, Five, and Six and more of a temporal link in Scene Three. In his last appearance, in Scene Seven, his roles as narrator and character finally merge.

As narrator at the start of the play Tom offers almost a textbook example of exposition: he informs us of what we need to know in order to understand the situation of the Wingfields, briefly sketching the geographical, social, and historical background of the action. From him we learn that the story is set in St Louis, Missouri; that the family belongs to the 'huge middle class of America' (the lower middle class, as we later come to realise); and that the time of the play, the late 1930s, is one of national difficulties ('a dissolving economy') and international uncertainties ('in Spain there was revolution'). Much the same information is restated in Tom's speech about the Paradise Dance Hall in Scene Five.

He also introduces the main characters, hinting at the tensions that may make them interesting and the problems that may develop into conflicts. Thus we learn early in Scene One that Amanda and her two children have been deserted by Mr Wingfield and that Jim, although a real character, should also be regarded as a symbol, 'the long delayed but always expected something that we live for'. Later, in Scene Six, Tom as narrator provides us with a full portrait of Jim O'Connor as a preface to Jim's actual appearance on the stage.

In addition, Tom's early comments tell us what kind of a play we are witnessing, providing an exposition of the play itself and its methods. His very first words warn us that it is the play's aim to portray truth, but that we will have to look for this truth beyond theatrical trickery and stage illusion. And a few paragraphs later he introduces the justification for the dim lighting and the background music (two essentially non-realistic elements) that contribute to the 'magic' of the stage presentation: this is to be 'a memory play'. In Scene Three, by contrast, the narrator functions rather as a temporal link between events that are otherwise distant in time. His words inform us of the lapse of time between Scene Two, a winter scene (notice Amanda's reproaches to Laura and Laura's sickness), and Scene Five, a spring scene (as announced by the stage direction, 'it is early dusk of a spring evening'). At the end of the play, the two functions are combined: as narrator, Tom tells us of the outcome of his relationship with his family; as character, he confesses the guilt he feels about abandoning them.

The device of the narrator clearly solves in part Williams's problem of exposition. Without it he could hardly have dramatised the socio-cultural, historical, and geographical background of his tale so early in the play and so economically; neither would one be so immediately aware of Amanda's personal plight. More obviously still, the portrait of Jim in Scene Six could not have been sketched in all its fine detail had Williams attempted to present it in dramatised form late in the play. Moreover, the narrator creates a temporal, historical perspective for events that are indeed 'memories'. Being himself an undisguised convention, he fits the style of the play and allows for a more flexible use of setting and a freer mode of presentation. In other words, as he steps in and out of the frame of the play proper, the narrator indicates that we are dealing with two periods distinct in time—the immediate present of the spectators, and the past of the play's events; moreover, he draws attention to the artificiality of the presentation to encourage us to direct our attention to the emotional truth behind it.

By choosing the narrator from among the characters, Williams integrates this figure more closely into the fabric of the play's events. As a character, Tom is also a participant; his report therefore acquires the ring of authenticity of the eyewitness account. With a narrator who is also a character we get the impression that we are closer to the reality of events, indeed to the truth.

But what is gained in vividness and immediacy must be paid for in other ways. As a participant in the events, Tom may have only a limited or strongly subjective view of them. What we see is in fact seen for us; it is what Tom chooses to show us, and we may have second thoughts about the reliability of the whole report. The method of presentation that Williams has adopted for his play is not, as critics have pointed out, without its inconsistencies, for if Tom is indeed the source of our information, we may well wonder how he himself acquired it. We might argue, for example, that although Tom did not actually witness the exchange between Amanda and Laura in Scene Two, he knows them intimately enough and may have gleaned sufficient information from either of them to piece the incident together in imagination. But could we justify in the same way his presentation of the scene in which Amanda and Laura prepare for the visitor, or of the protracted interview between Laura and the gentleman caller?

In all fairness it should be said here that the play emphatically rejects realistic conventions, and that this kind of logical objection should not therefore be raised against it. Moreover, and this may well be the ultimate argument, in performance the impression of seeing the action from a temporal distance through Tom's memory dissipates as soon as the fourth wall ascends out of sight, and we are emotionally drawn into the play to the extent that we forget about the technicalities of its presentation.

Characters and characterisation

The Glass Menagerie belongs to the broad category of psychological drama. It does not start out with a message; it does not purport to demonstrate a point. Nor does it conclude with a firm recommendation or a verdict. If anything, it teaches understanding of, and compassion for, all four of its protagonists rather than for a single character. The strength of the play is its sensitive creation of characters with whom audiences the world over can identify or sympathise. Williams is not a preacher; he does not use the stage as a pulpit to deliver moral lessons. Through his characters and their story, however, he raises questions that haunt us all: How do we live? What are our values? Why do we act the way we do? Can we be true to ourselves and considerate of the needs of others at the same time?

In his introductory speech Tom states that he has 'a poet's weakness for symbols'. The whole play, including the characters, should be viewed not as a realistic or naturalistic 'slice of life', a photographically accurate presentation of 'life in the late thirties', but as an imaginative and poetic reconstruction of personal memories. Therefore, the student should be alert to the manner as much as to the matter, to characterisation as much as to character. In this section we will consider each character in succession, adopting the point of view of the spectator and looking at their physical appearances, dialogue and actions.

This is how an audience generally discovers characters as the play unfolds: through what they look like, what they say, what they do, and what others say about them. A work of literature rarely develops in the linear fashion of a play in production. When we read or see a play for the first time we are more sensitive to those aspects that appear perfectly realistic. As the drama progresses, what seemed at first perfectly simple or even trivial and irrelevant acquires a deeper resonance. By the time the curtain falls, this new meaning may have supplanted the initial straightforward significance. Upon subsequent reading or viewing, the play will have acquired a different value and may reveal further riches. The student of drama must, then, necessarily adopt an ambiguous position: he must retain the fresh approach of his first experience to let the play progressively reveal its strengths and emphases; at the same time, however, he must be fully aware of later developments in order to discern the skill with which he is being led through the play and the particular meaning of that dramatic itinerary.

The father: a photograph

The father of the Wingfield family does not actually appear on the stage, but he is present in the text of the play from the narrator's introductory words ('There is a fifth character in the play'; p.23) to his final speech ('I left Saint Louis . . . and followed, from then on, in my father's footsteps', p.115). His physical absence is compensated for by the allusions to him that appear in practically every scene and by the blown-up photograph in the living room, in which he appears in a doughboy's First World War cap.

In the course of the play, Amanda stops in front of the picture several times as she reminisces about her husband's charm (p.27), her love for him (p.50), and their first meeting in Blue Mountain amid the jonquils (p.72). For her the picture represents the great love of her life transformed by memory into an eternally young and handsome soldier. But in at least one instance, (p.82), when entertaining Jim O'Connor with her stories of a long-gone South (p.82), she feels uncomfortable about the picture of the smiling gentleman. In the apartment where she has painstakingly tried to recreate the illusion of elegance and gentility to trap a young man into marrying her daughter—to make a gentleman caller into a husband, as the constant juxtaposition of the two motifs reminds us—the husband's grinning portrait both mocks her scheme and offers an uncomfortable prophecy that her past failure to keep a husband will be repeated in her failure to secure a mate for Laura.

To Tom, the picture of his father represents not the past but the future. The tone of his description of the portrait in his introductory speech, both admiring and flippant, foreshadows his eventual imitation of his father. The similarity of their natures and, the play suggests, of their destinies, is emphasised by using in the production a photograph of the actor playing Tom. In the course of the action Tom refers to his father's picture explicitly only once, in his drunken report in Scene Four of the magician's trick that impressed him so much. 'Who in hell ever got himself out of a [nailed-up] coffin?' he asks Laura, and on the back wall, 'as if in answer, the father's grinning photograph lights up' (p.46). The device may seem over-obvious in preparing the audience for Tom's final departure, but the unchanged grin, revealed in full light, may also represent an ironical comment. The doughboy's First World War cap should remind us that if Tom chooses to follow the example of his father, he might well find the adventurous life of which he dreams as a soldier in the Second World War.

Amanda's and Tom's relationship to the portrait, then, is ambiguous. Evoking a beloved memory for Amanda, it is also a foreboding omen of renewed disillusionment; embodying a dream of adventure for Tom, it also foreshadows new entrapment. It is symptomatic that Laura, in a world apart from that of Tom or her mother, does not refer to the portrait at all.

Amanda Wingfield

Amanda is the dominating figure of the play. Her name, the Latin word for 'worthy of being loved', expresses one of her essential traits, her need to give and receive love. This need appears throughout the play and especially in her evocation of the crowd of prominent young planters that were her suitors (pp.26–7): 'Her eyes lift, her face glows, her voice becomes rich and elegiac.' Conversely, her name also suggests that when she feels deprived of loving regard—as is the case in the play —she may turn into, in Tom's words, an unattractive 'ugly—babbling old—*witch*' (p.42). The two aspects of Amanda's personality embedded in her name are already traceable in the unusually long description of her in the playwright's list of characters (p.5), where she is presented as the prototype of the Williams heroine, torn between present and past. Like the lives of Myra in *Battle of Angels* (1939), Blanche DuBois in *A Streetcar Named Desire* (1948), Serafina delle Rose in *The Rose Tattoo* (1951), her life is characterised by an intense emotional experience followed by an abrupt decline precipitated by the loss of a life-mate, and like them she tries desperately to recapture an earlier time.

Amanda and the South
Amanda is often described as a person immersed in the past, bewildered by her immediate surroundings, unable to cope with the social and economic reality of the Depression days, and constantly taking refuge

in memories of bygone greatness connected with her adolescence and early adulthood in the South. For Amanda, the South is the lost paradise of her Blue Mountain youth, revealed indirectly and in brief glimpses throughout the play. Amanda's descriptions of her past weave a picture of a graceful, genteel Old South dominated by refined social gatherings and elegant living conditions. She reminisces fondly about leading a cotillion, winning the cakewalk twice at Sunset Hill, and attending the Governor's ball in Jackson (p.71). She waxes rhapsodic about spring pastimes—evening dances, long rides, picnics in the Mississippi Delta region (p.72). Her most compelling recollection of the past is that in which she emerges as the most sought-after girl in the Delta, with seventeen gentlemen callers on the same Sunday afternoon (p.26).

Amanda's vibrant memories of that Arcadian South are qualified by a few sombre touches. The names of places connected with her past introduce the first sobering hints. With its aura of physical and geographical unreality, the name 'Blue Mountain' seems designed to imply that—at least in the context of the play—Amanda's story belongs to the realm of fairy tale. Her introductory phrase, 'One Sunday afternoon in Blue Mountain' (p.26), clearly reminds us of the 'once upon a time' of legendary stories and reinforces the impression of unreality. 'Sunset Hill', moreover, introduces a nostalgic suggestion of things once brilliant but now slowly fading, perhaps dimmed by distance in time.

The ideal vision of the South is also tarnished by Amanda's reference to the callousness with which elderly unmarried relatives (and presumably all who did not conform to the prevailing social norms) were treated. The idyllic picture is further marred by the intrusion of death, which has taken its toll among Amanda's former admirers. After her long inventory of rich and handsome suitors Tom enquires sarcastically of the last one mentioned, 'What did he leave his widow?'—a question which pointedly emphasises the almost complete disappearance of the human background of his mother's youth. By its very length, Amanda's catalogue of departed suitors hints, beyond the personal tragedies, at the waning of a way of life, that of the planters' aristocracy, and the decay of a society, that of the Old South.

Against this background of social decline, in an atmosphere of lust for life and morbid fascinations, amid young men dying violent deaths in futile quarrels, Amanda's infatuation and eventual marriage to Mr Wingfield became just another example of the rapidly disintegrating structure of the society in which she grew up. Her enthusiasm and elation in reporting the exciting meeting with her future husband should not obscure the fact that her marriage was a breach of the code regulating such arrangements. The efficiency of the rules that had ensured continuity in the past, invoked by Amanda herself as justification for her interest in Jim O'Connor's background, is again sarcastically questioned by Tom: 'Then how did you happen to make a tragic mistake?' Amanda has to concede that 'the innocent look of [Mr Wingfield] had everyone fooled!' (p.64). Tom's critical attitude and Amanda's wistful answer underline the fact that even in the heyday of her youth the careful regulation of refined Southern society was disintegrating. Moreover, the union of a girl representing the predominantly past-oriented agrarian South with a travelling telephone-company man, an exponent of the contemporary technological world, contributes to the picture of the Old South slowly giving way under the pressure of the twentieth century.

Amanda's escapism

Amanda's retreat into memories of the past, her backward glance, is only one aspect of her imaginative way of dismissing the present; the other consists of averting her gaze from her surroundings and, more often than not, looking forward to hypothetical happiness in the future.

Characteristic of this escapism is Amanda's refusal to acknowledge that Laura is peculiar psychologically (p.66); more surprisingly, she even blots out the fact of Laura's physical defect by refusing to call her 'crippled' (p.35, p.65). She protests that her son is not merely a clerk in a warehouse and transmutes both her children against all evidence into people 'full of endowments' (p.49). This pathetic overstatement reveals her proud motherly love as much as her refusal to face life squarely. In spite of constant proof to the contrary provided by her daily life she continues to believe the slogan 'try and you will *succeed*' (p.49), a motto which reveals, as Gerald Weales has pointed out, as blatant an acceptance of the American success myth as Willy Loman's in *Death of a Salesman*.

Amanda's attempt to fly from her depressing tenement life to an idyllic, rosy future is manifest again in the short episode on the fire-escape landing in Scene Five in which the mother, looking at the new moon, expresses her wish for 'success and happiness' (p.58). The moon denotes the unrealisable aspirations of the character that stares at it. Amanda's wish, like the far-away orb, is unattainable. Notice that Tom characteristically introduces a deflating comment about the moon, pointing out its position above the urban Jewish delicatessen, and then proceeds ironically to interpret his mother's grandiloquent prayer as a substitute 'wish for a gentleman caller' (p.58). His remarks indicate his detached attitude towards his mother's sentimentality and romantic dreaming.

Amanda's self-defeat

When the gentleman caller is about to arrive, when the dream of the future seems about to be realised, Amanda defeats her own purpose by suddenly reverting to her past. Both the refurbishing of the house and the 'resurrection' of the dress are attempts to conceal her shabby present and recapture part of the elegance she associates with her Blue Mountain days. Amanda's knack for entertaining, her outgoing manner, her conversational talents, while underscoring by contrast Laura's defects, soon charm the visitor, who 'after the first shock . . . reacts very warmly—grins and chuckles, is altogether won over' (p.81). Amanda has thus vicariously seduced the man for herself. By becoming for that one evening the girl she once was, Amanda has unwittingly made the occasion a losing battle for Laura. Amanda's 'plans and provisions' (p.52) go up in smoke.

The set and the lighting accentuate the irony of the situation. At centre stage, in full light, Amanda gaily relives her past moments of glory. Jim and Tom are captivated. At stage left, in shadow, Laura lies silent and petrified on the sofa, clenching her hand to her lips to hold back a shuddering sob (p.84). This tableau, then, shows more immediately and more movingly than words that Laura's anxiety and withdrawal have probably been caused, or at least heightened, by Amanda's remarkable social charm. Of this Amanda remains forever unaware. After her great scene with the gentleman caller, she disappears from view. When she emerges again, at the very end of the play, it is to acknowledge that she has made 'a fool of herself' (p.113). But by shifting the blame to Tom's selfishness and his ignorance of the fact that Jim was already engaged to be married, she allows herself to disregard her own self-centredness and the determining role she has played in this particular fiasco and—the whole play now seems to suggest—in the larger human failure of Laura.

Amanda's stature as a character

Amanda is one of the most memorable female characters in Tennessee Williams's work and indeed in the whole of modern theatre. The author describes her sympathetically in his preliminary list of characters as 'a little woman of great but confused vitality clinging frantically to another time and place . . . There is much to admire in Amanda, and as much to love and pity as there is to laugh at. Certainly she has endurance and a kind of heroism, and though her foolishness makes her unwittingly cruel at times, there is tenderness in her slight person' (p.5). Most of the time she appears as a silly old woman, ranting about her past; her blind devotion to her children suffocates them and her narrow-minded moral outlook makes her harsh at times. But throughout the play, she remains aware in thought and deed of what her life is. She points out to Tom that 'life's not easy, it calls for—Spartan endurance!' (p.50) and later that 'the future becomes the present, the present the past and the past turns into everlasting regret if you don't plan for it!' (p.63). In this awareness of life as a struggle and in her acceptance of it on these terms resides Amanda's claim to our admiration. However unreasonable her demands, grotesque her nervous gaiety, or vulgar her mercantilism, they are all superseded by the fighting spirit, the bravura, and the sheer will to overcome harboured in her small frame.

In the epilogue, Amanda is seen 'as though viewed through sound-proof glass . . . making a comforting speech to Laura . . . Now that we cannot hear the mother's speech, her silliness is gone and she has dignity and tragic beauty' (p.114). In this ultimate pantomime is thus confirmed what makes Amanda eminently human and lovable and what it is that justifies her name. Amanda's dignity and endearing loveliness grow from her uncommon endurance in the face of adversity, from her courage to continue to strive for a dream which is unattainable yet worthy, a dream of the past and the future, shattered by reality, but never quite forgotten or forgone.

Tom Wingfield

Tom is, to a large extent, a portrait of the artist as a young man. Williams's description of him in the introductory list of characters provides the key to Tom's whole personality: 'His nature is not remorseless, but to escape from a trap he has to act without pity' (p.5). The desire to escape from the various figurative prisons that threaten to engulf him is the deep-seated motive that prompts all of Tom's actions in the play and renders them consistent.

Tom at the warehouse

The most obvious trap from which Tom is trying to escape is his job at the warehouse, to which he feels chained as the sole provider for his family. To someone like Tom, who holds with D.H. Lawrence that 'man is by instinct a lover, a hunter, a fighter' (p.52), the warehouse is a veritable cage that shackles all basic impulses. This appears clearly in Tom's description of his job in Scene Three. The ugliness of the industrial setting, the numbingly repetitive activity, and the alienating effect of the job, turn the warehouse into a box in which Tom experiences death-in-life. Notice his revealing statement: 'I'd rather somebody picked up a crowbar and battered out my brains—than go back mornings!' (p.41).

The warehouse, then, is a prison in which he and his companions of the lower middle class, 'this largest and fundamentally enslaved section of American society', are forced to 'exist and function as one interfused mass of automatism' (p.21). The confinement in the warehouse is worse for Tom because he is a poet, unlike his co-workers. He reports that his companions, at first hostile and suspicious, gradually grew more toler-ant of him but never got beyond considering him 'an oddly fashioned dog who trots across their path at some distance' (p.69). The same combination of benevolence and irony is traceable in the nickname 'Shakespeare' (p.68) given Tom by Jim. The alienation and the isolation that characterise Tom's situation at the warehouse are restated near the end of the play when, defending himself against Amanda's re-proaches about the gentleman caller, Tom remarks, 'the warehouse is where I work, not where I know things about people' (p.113). From this industrial version of the concentration camp, Tom seeks escape in literary activity. By day he retires 'to a cabinet of the washroom to work on poems' (p.68). His refuge, hardly a place conducive to poetic inspiration, provides an ironic comment on the whole situation: literary work even here is better than the activity in the warehouse!

Tom at home

By night Tom would likewise escape into his poetic world were it not that Amanda's anxiety about his health—prompted both by motherly solicitude and by fear for the family's sole source of income—prevents any creative concentration. Amanda's sermons to Tom at the table and her 'hawklike attention to every bite he takes' (p.24) not only spoil his meals but help to make 'home' a cage as oppressive as the warehouse.

Amanda's over-protective attitude naturally extends to clothing. As Tom is about to leave for the warehouse after yet another painful con-versation with his mother in Scene Four she requests that he 'put his wool muffler on', whereupon Tom 'snatches it angrily from the closet and tosses it around his neck and pulls both ends tight' (p.54). The gesture may well be meant as a sarcastic simulation of Amanda's stifling influence on his life.

Another episode connected with clothes also exemplifies Amanda's mothering role and Tom's growing impatience with it. After the violent quarrel of Scene Three, in which Tom compares his mother to a witch, Amanda grabs his arm as he tries to get past her. Tom screams at her 'Don't grab at me, mother!' but catches his arm in the sleeve of the coat that he is struggling to put on. The stage direction informs us that 'he tears the coat off again splitting the shoulder of it, and hurls it across the room against the fragile collection of Laura's glass animals' (p.42). The whole action shows the confinement of Tom's life and his mother's active role in it, foreshadowing the cruel action of escape that will later become necessary. Tom's helpless kneeling beside the scattered debris also hints at the remorse which will haunt him after his departure, a remorse which he acknowledges in his last speech as narrator (p.115).

Tom's self-reproaches, another aspect of the prison-like atmosphere that surrounds him, are grounded in Amanda's belief that he has a moral obligation to serve as substitute head of the family. Sharing with Tom her apprehensions about Laura's future, Amanda sets down as the condition for his release the finding of a suitable husband for his sister: 'as soon as Laura has got somebody to take care of her, married, a home of her own, independent—why then you'll be free to go wherever you please' (p.53). Laura is thus made by her mother into another stifling element of Tom's prison. But the real agent of confinement is Amanda, and the cage of Tom's moral obligation is made all the more binding through her self-effacement—'I don't say me because I'm old and don't matter! I say for your sister because she's young and dependent' (p.53)—and her ostentatious show of solicitude for Laura.

Tom's routes of escape
Caught in Amanda's moral blackmail, Tom in one instance angrily draws a world in which he fancies himself as all-powerful, and where his current imposed behaviour and morality are smashed. This flight of his imagination, inspired less by Tom's real dream than by a desire to oppose and hurt his mother, is contained in the violent outburst against Amanda that immediately precedes his breaking of Laura's figurines. With his evocation of the underworld, Tom blasts at the heart of his mother's dreams. For her 'gentle South' he substitutes a brutal, insensitive northern gang culture; for the halcyon plantation life, a battering urban vision. Notice, however, that in spite of this clash of dreams, both mother and son resort to basically the same escape mechanism to blot out an oppressive reality.

Another example of Tom's attempt to escape from his prison, even temporarily, is his frequent filmgoing. The 'shower of movie-ticket stubs' that falls to the ground as he rummages through his pocket to find his key belies Amanda's suspicion that 'Nobody goes to the movies night after night. Nobody in their right mind goes to the movies as often as you pretend to' (p.41). Tom's addiction to films spotlights the intensity of his restlessness and the increasing difficulty he experiences in controlling it. The 'narcotic of the cinema', as one critic has called it, coupled with bouts of heavy drinking, lets him forget temporarily the oppression of the apartment. He tastes adventure vicariously, becoming a hero at the cinema as he never can at home. His report to Laura at the start of Scene Four on 'the very long programme' and the Malvolio show (pp.44–5) recaptures the essentials of his situation. The financial hardships of the Great Depression, the confinement in the warehouse, the smothering affection of his mother, the moral obligation to his sister, the frustration of his poetic ambitions—all are likened to a living death, an entrapment in a nailed-up coffin. The allusion to the coffin on one hand and the lighted portrait on the other poses Tom's dilemma in drastically clear scenic terms as a choice between death and escape.

For the attentive reader, however, Williams has introduced a skilfully managed touch of dramatic irony. From the start we have been given indications that Tom will not be able to imitate the actor's nonviolent escape in real life. The first words of the Prologue—'I am the opposite of a stage magician'—clearly exclude the possibility that Tom will ever be able to emulate Malvolio's trick.

Much the same meaning is implicit in Williams's decision to have Tom wear a sailor's outfit in both the Prologue and the Epilogue. Exhibited at the very beginning of the play, the sailor's clothes have a prophetic value. They announce that despite the various prisons that threaten to detain him, Tom will ultimately manage to 'escape into freedom' and accomplish the destiny that he imagines is before him. His outfit, then, stresses the inevitability of the play's outcome. But the precise nature of the costume (in the acting version specifically described as consisting of a pea jacket and a watch cap, both garments designed to protect sailors in foul weather) indicates that Tom's freedom is 'an ambiguous one, that the romantic dream of escaping into a world of freedom and large vistas' announced by the projected image of a 'Sailing Vessel with Jolly Roger' has been deflated. The universe into which Tom has escaped is described in the Epilogue as a world of alienation, uprootedness, and loneliness. Instead of freedom at sea, Tom has merely found the cold and hostile world of harbours swept by winter and the lonely, aimless wandering of the dispossessed.

The final irony comes with Tom's rueful concluding acknowledgment that he has escaped one prison only to fall into another, that of his guilty conscience, his memories of home, the glass animals and quaint melodies, his sister's gaze. From Prologue to Epilogue Tom thus emerges, like Amanda in her yellow dress, as a dreamer whose romantic visions, although destroyed by reality, linger hauntingly in his consciousness.

Laura Wingfield

Laura is the most pathetic figure of the play. A good deal of her character is expressed in the connotations of the nickname 'Blue Roses' given her in high school by Jim. The unusual combination of words epitomises Laura's whole being. Through its association with the colour blue, the rose is here deprived of its traditional overtone of passion, as is Laura, but it acquires an aura of strangeness and uniqueness which subtly renders the fragile prettiness of the girl and, at the same time, her alienation and estrangement, her difference from the others, her vital inadequacy. Moreover, playing on another meaning of 'blue' Williams here suggests the atmosphere of sadness and melancholy that envelops Laura's slight, hardly real person.

If we turn from Laura's nickname to her physical appearance we find many of these suggestions restated and confirmed. Laura's dress in Scene Two, as described by Williams, adds to the overtones conveyed by her nickname and associates her with yet another flower. In the beginning of the scene, Laura is seen seated in a delicate ivory chair at a small claw-foot table, wearing a kimono of soft violet material. Recalling the violet, a flower which traditionally symbolises modesty, the colour of Laura's dress combines with the daintiness of the furniture to surround her with fragility and shyness. The delicacy with which Laura's association with flowers endows her is again evoked in her confession that she had sought refuge from business school in 'that big glass house where they raise the tropical flowers' at the zoo.

Laura's strangeness and vulnerability are further presented as the accelerating factor of her separation from the world. Her limp is the outward sign that marks her as one of those whose excessive sensitivity exposes them to symbolic mutilation in an unfeeling modern world. Laura's brace is the mechanical device that remedies the physical defect but aggravates the moral damage. In high school, as she tells Jim, arriving late for class was humiliating because she imagined that the clumping of the brace attracted everybody's attention to her limp. Laura's physical defect and the mechanical remedy, her limp and her brace, have been identified by many critics as symbols of Amanda's influence on her daughter. Nancy Tischler remarks, for example, that 'It is Amanda's forcefulness that allows Laura to walk at all, but it is also Amanda's example that discourages Laura from walking naturally.'*

Laura's relationship with Amanda
During the elaborate preparation in Scene Six for the gentleman caller's visit, an event engineered to remedy Laura's inability to make social contacts, Amanda produces 'two powder puffs which she wraps in handkerchiefs and stuffs in Laura's bosom' (p.70) to cover up another of the girl's physical deficiencies: 'to be painfully honest, your chest is flat'. But instead of boosting Laura's morale, instead of easing her tension and steadying her delicate balance, all the preparations seem instead to reduce her meagre natural resources and to upset her inner poise.

Amanda's 'bracing' of her daughter finally brings the girl to a state of terror that ultimately defeats the purpose of the gentleman caller's visit. Amanda's social skills contrast unfortunately with Laura's awkwardness. Amanda is a natural hostess; Laura is retiring and shy. This painful difference is evident yet again in a small incident connected with clothes. At one point, Laura puts on 'a shapeless felt hat' and her

*In *Tennessee Williams: Rebellious Puritan*, The Citadel Press, New York, 1965, p.99.

mother's 'inaccurately made-over coat, the sleeves too short for Laura' (p.47) to go out to the neighbourhood delicatessen on an errand. The poorly fitting garment on Laura's back represents an unsuccessful attempt to don a personality not her own, to adopt ideas alien to her nature in the hope of coping more adequately with the outside world.

It is symptomatic of her failure in this respect that, as she steps out of apartment in her mother's clothes, she slips on the landing of the fire escape and almost hurts herself seriously (p.47). This seemingly unimportant incident shows that Laura can exist in relative safety on only one level of reality, that of the apartment with her music and glass figurines. Contrary to Amanda's belief that 'Sticks and stones can break our bones, but the expression on Mr Garfinkel's face won't harm us!' (p.47), the hostile reception of an insensitive world—'Mother, they make such faces when I ask them to charge it'—is as painful to Laura as a real fracture.

Another instance of Amanda's ambivalent role in Laura's life is provided by the episode at Rubicam Business College. Here again, Amanda promotes a project financed by the subscription campaign money and designed to transmute Laura, if she cannot be a Southern belle, a wife, and a mother, into a career girl. But Laura cannot cope with the mechanisation of the contemporary world represented by the weekly speed test on the typewriter any more than she can bear the mercenary insensitivity on Mr Garfinkel's face. The first makes her sick; the second causes her to fall.

Laura's refuges: The victrola, the glass animals, and others

The scratchy, old-fashioned music of the gramophone presents Laura with her own world of sounds, her private shelter against the noise of the Paradise Dance Hall. A recognisable offspring of the past-oriented Amanda, Laura takes refuge from the hot swing music and the staccato rhythms of the industrial world in the sentimental melodies of the 1920s. The tunes that are Laura's musical refuge, although different from the melody that serves as a leitmotif for the play as a whole, share some of its characteristics. The girl's preference for the music of the past implies a movement away from actuality that recalls the music-from-afar quality of the leitmotif melody. These tunes, moreover, are recorded on 'those worn-out phonograph records her father left as a painful reminder of him' (p.34). It is thus hinted that Laura's retreat into the music and her huddling beside the old victrola may be part of an unconscious search for a father, her instinctive quest for protection against her overpowering mother.

The role of the melodies as a refuge is underlined once again when Laura must confront the gentleman caller, the representative of a world from which she flees. As the doorbell rings, the tension that has been building up is too much for her and she begs Amanda not to make her go to the door. When Amanda finally orders her to 'march right to that door!' (p.75), the stage direction notes that 'A faraway, scratchy rendition of Dardanella softens the air and gives her strength to move through it. She slips to the door and draws it cautiously open' (p.76). The opening of the door acquires here a symbolic significance that transcends the mere gesture of welcome. Laura is afraid to let the outsider into her life. The outcome shows her apprehension to have been instinctively right.

Laura's is a universe not only of sound but of glass, centring on the collection of figurines announced in the title. She withdraws to the company of her little animals whenever the outside world becomes threatening. When Amanda mentions the possibility of marriage, a stage direction specifies that 'Laura utters a startled, doubtful laugh. She reaches quickly for a piece of glass' (p.35), seeking protection from her mother's suggestion of matrimony in the tactile comfort of her figurines.

Laura's retreat to a dark corner of the stage, her huddling amidst inanimate objects which she endows with imaginary existence, is indicative of her movement away from real life, of the 'separation' that Williams mentions in his initial description of her and ultimately of her unfitness for existence. That suggestion is further reinforced by her identification with the thirteen-year-old glass unicorn, the figurine dearest to her.

Laura talks about the unicorn with warmth and sympathy, admitting that its singularity may make it feel lonesome and uncomfortable in a world which, as the playwright says, attempts to reduce living creatures to automatons. Her warning to Jim—'Oh, be careful—if you breathe, it breaks!' (p.101)—may well imply that since the unicorn is only an imaginary creature, the act of breathing (a basic manifestation of real life) might be too much of a test for it, as it is in a different sense for her. The unicorn, even more than the glass collection as a whole, is a perfect symbol for Laura. To the characteristic fragility and delicate beauty possessed by all glass figurines, it adds the quality of uniqueness and, as a consequence, almost of freakishness. In it are thus extended the various implications of Laura's nickname, 'Blue Roses'.

The world of music and glass which Laura superimposes on her surroundings conceals their shabbiness from her. Since she shares neither her brother's desire to escape nor her mother's dream of retrieved gentility, the apartment, for her, is not a prison. It is protective and pacifying. Thus the opening of Scene Two, which reveals her alone at home in her dainty chair with her violet dress, washing and polishing her collection of glass to the sound of her favourite music (p.29), provides a picture of perfect serenity. This is the only scene in which Laura seems to attain a quiet happiness.

When her mother's misdirected ambition forces her into the world of business, and when the weekly speed test proves to be more than she can take, Laura, looking for the shelter she usually finds in the company of her little glass animals, seeks refuge at the city zoo. Here again she is unaware of the unpleasant aspect of the place, with its caged inhabitants; to her the cage is rather a means of protection against a threatening outside world. The penguins, her favourite animals, are no less revealing of Laura's deep-seated feelings of inadequacy than is her little unicorn. In them, she unconsciously sees reflected her own limp and general helplessness. She feels akin to them and pathetically states that she visited them every day.

Her other refuge at the zoo, the 'jewel-box', 'that big glass house where they raise the tropical flowers' (p.33), obliquely illustrates another aspect of Laura. Her prediliction for the hothouse again implies that she is a beautiful but fragile plant, too frail for the 'winter of the cities' world that her mother describes on learning of her truancy: 'Walking? In winter? Deliberately courting pneumonia in that light coat?' (p.32). When forced to leave the protective apartment for the ugly world of the city, Laura thus instinctively finds her way back to a substitute refuge, a place where she feels comfortable.

The absence in Laura's mind of a resentment comparable to her brother's or an ambition like her mother's, and her indifference to life outside the apartment, are clearly brought out in the episode in which Amanda, elated by her conversation with Tom about a possible gentleman caller, calls Laura out of the kitchen to express her deepest yearnings by wishing on the moon. Amanda's forceful, almost physical insistence elicits only a bewildered reaction from her dreamy daughter, for whom the door that Tom has left open on the outside world exerts less of a fascination than the beloved interior from which she is dragged away. Laura's genuine puzzlement establishes that her mother's aspirations are completely foreign to her quietly serene and contented nature.

When Jim intrudes upon her life and that of the household, he will for a moment throw open the door to replace the old-fashioned music with that coming from the Paradise Dance Hall, and the fragile glow of the glass menagerie with the tinselly cheap flashes of the large glass sphere that hangs from the ceiling there. After his departure, darkness sets in over the remnants of the glass animals: Laura is irremediably broken for having opened the door of her life to let in a representative of the modern mechanised world.

The gentleman caller: Jim O'Connor

The name of the gentleman caller, Jim D. O'Connor, establishes him at the very start as an Irishman. 'The D. is for Delaney', Tom says, eliciting

Amanda's exclamation, 'Irish on *both* sides! *Gracious!* And doesn't drink?' (p.63). More than a preconceived idea about the Irish as a people, Amanda's remark expresses her fear of marrying her daughter to a drunkard like her own husband. Later in the play, her exclamation acquires ironic overtones: in her eagerness to find a suitable partner for Laura she has overlooked a far more obvious obstacle to the marriage than the one brought to her mind by the mention of Jim's name.

Jim is described in the introductory remarks as 'a nice, ordinary, young man' (p.5). In the scene with Laura he is comically identified with a large ruminant as he reflectively chews gum, declaring that he feels 'comfortable as a cow' (p.90). The image conveys Jim's tremendous good nature and gentle humour, but juxtaposed with Laura's shelves of dainty glass figurines, it also suggests a massive insensitivity as compared to the girl's delicate fragility.

Another trait of Jim's physique further stresses the radical contrast between Jim and Laura while simultaneously hinting at an ultimate resemblance between them. His fellow worker, Tom says, has 'the scrubbed and polished look of white chinaware' (p.68). More explicitly still, in his scene with Laura, Jim states, 'I'm not made out of glass' (p.102). The unexpected comparison to chinaware deprives Jim of the shining prettiness conveyed by the imagery of glass surrounding Laura, endowing him instead with the dull, attenuated radiance of the common kitchen dish and reducing him to the ordinary boy that he is. Although the image of chinaware reveals in Jim a kind of commonness and ordinariness, a fibre coarser than Laura's, it nevertheless introduces an overtone of fragility perhaps less conspicuous but equally real. Though Jim may not, as he unequivocally states, be made out of glass, he is all the same breakable.

Jim and the American Dream

In Tom's opening speech, Jim is described as 'the most realistic character in the play, being an emissary from a world of reality that we were somehow set apart from' (p.23). The 'world of reality' ushered in by Jim is presented less as the real world of the late 1930s than as a caricature of the American Dream by a shallow, selfish materialist. For Jim, the industrial world of the warehouse is neither an environment that stifles his deeper personal aspirations nor a milieu alienating him from his fellow man. It is not a prison for the 'enslaved' lower middle class but that class's 'rung on the ladder towards success'.* It is symptomatic that while Tom should feel 'an oddly fashioned dog' (p.69) without any point of contact with his fellow workers, Jim has the ear and is the confidant of Mr Mendoza, the foreman.

*Stein, Roger B.: '*The Glass Menagerie* Revisited: Catastrophe without Violence'. *Western Humanities Review* 18 (Spring 1964), pp.141–53.

As a confirmed advocate of the American Dream, Jim is also a great believer in self-improvement through education and has therefore enrolled in a course in public speaking that 'fits you for—executive positions!' (p.77). The lecture on self-confidence, delivered for the benefit of a wondering and mildly bewildered Laura (pp.98-9), is nothing more than an expansion of the cliché which Amanda had earlier urged upon Tom: 'Try and you will *succeed*' (p.49). Jim's infatuation with the dream of a better, greater, and richer life for all is further manifested in his admiration for the Wrigley Building in Chicago and the 'fortune made by the guy that invented the first piece of chewing gum' (p.90). His enthusiastic account of the Hall of Science at the Century of Progress exhibition implies a blind faith in the possibility of infinite material progress secured by technological advances. Jim's ardent profession of faith in electrodynamics builds to a climax: 'Full steam— [His eyes are starry] *Knowledge*—zzzzp! *Money*—Zzzzzzp!—*Power*! That's the cycle democracy is built on! (p.100).

Yet for all its convincing dynamism, Jim's advocacy of the American Dream is full of ironic touches. The discrepancy between his 'strident theme of success' and the less glamorous reality before us is underlined by his own mention of an 'America even more wonderful than the present' in a household composed of a son who is 'a poet with a job in a warehouse' and who plunges the family into darkness because he refused to pay the light bill; a mother, a relic of a brilliant past, who is forced to sell magazine subscriptions and ladies' underwear to make both ends meet; and a daughter whose shyness prevents her from confronting the outside world—all haunted by the memory of a father who was an undistinguished telephone man before he deserted them. Adding further to the irony is the fact that Jim himself seems to have experienced the acme of his dream of success in the past, during his high school days.

An image projected on a screen on the stage obtrusively presents Jim as a 'High School Hero' (p.68), while Tom, as narrator, offers the following introduction: 'In high school Jim was a hero . . . He seemed to move in a continual spotlight. He was a star in basketball, captain of the debating club, president of the senior class and the glee club and he sang the male lead in the annual light operas. He was always running or bounding, never just walking. He seemed always at the point of defeating the law of gravity' (p.68). From Tom's description Jim emerges as the prototype of the 'up and coming American boy'. Naturally energetic, athletically inclined, scholastically gifted, socially popular, Jim 'was shooting with such velocity through his adolescence that you would logically expect him to arrive at nothing short of the White House by the time he was thirty' (p.68). Yet even as Jim's vitality erupts on stage, a series of qualifying touches become apparent.

Even during Tom's presentation, the image on the screen switches from the 'High School Hero' to a mere 'clerk' (p.68), emphasising the idea of decline. In the course of Jim's conversation with Tom it becomes apparent that the former 'captain of the debating club' now needs to take up 'a course in public speaking' (p.77), and that instead of the presidential mansion in Washington he has to make do with a dingy St Louis factory office. All this irony is recaptured in the incident in which he and Laura read *The Torch* together. Jim's high school successes are recorded in the school yearbook, which Jim himself regards with nostalgia. When Laura produces the bound volume Jim exclaims, 'Holy Jeez! *The Torch*!', and the stage direction directs him to accept it reverently (p.95). The very name *The Torch* evokes Jim's flamboyant Promethean youth. But now, as he enters Laura's life for the second time, he is merely carrying an 'old candelabrum melted out of shape' whose few candles produce only a 'flickering light' (p.88). The ironic contrast is underlined when Jim, seated next to the feeble source of light and unaware of the pathetic touch of irony, describes himself as 'in the limelight' (p.90). The gap between the Promethean youth and the shoe-factory clerk, between the intense spotlight outlining the youthful star and the dim candlelight illuminating the gentleman caller, is the stark gulf between promise and actuality. When he hears that Laura wanted him to autograph her copy of *The Torch* but never could summon up the courage to approach him about it, Jim takes the book from her and signs it with a flourish. In so doing he reveals not only his appreciation of Laura's belatedly expressed admiration but also his nostalgic desire to cast himself in the glorious role once again. Through this episode Jim indirectly shows himself to be as much a dreamer as Amanda. The satisfaction he receives from reliving his high-school past parallels Amanda's elation at recalling her Blue Mountain days, and his declaration that one day his signature may be worth something parallels her hope for future material security.

Tom's statement that 'I was valuable to [Jim] as someone who could remember his former glory, who had seen him win basketball games and the silver cup in debating' (p.68) introduces by implication the growing inferiority complex that Jim bluntly acknowledges later in the play: 'You know what I judge to be the trouble with you? Inferiority complex! Know what that is? That's what they call it when someone low-rates himself! I understand it because I had it, too' (p.98). Although Jim goes on finding reasons for his not feeling that way any more and for his thinking of himself as of a superior being, the end of the speech contains some revealing stage directions: '[Unconsciously glances at himself in the mirror] All you've got to do is discover in *what* [you are superior]! Take me, for instance. [He adjusts his tie at the mirror]' (p.99). Beyond his evident narcissism and self-centredness, Jim obliquely shows through his furtive look in the mirror that he needs the reassurance of his looks and neatly-groomed attire.

Six years of fading illusions and dimming popularity, six years of 'running into interference' (p.68) have brought Jim to doubt, in the innermost recess of his psyche, the possibility of the brilliant future he was once promised. He is not broken but the crack is clearly perceptible. Even while he enunciates the method that might still lead him to the top, he cannot help taking into account that after all that time he is still 'planning to get in on the ground floor' (p.100). His glance at the mirror, then, is an attempt to quell the fears and doubts that rise in him even as he tries to plant some self-confidence in Laura.

Jim, Laura, and the unicorn

Turning from his own uncertain image in the mirror to the strange girl in front of him, the representative of the outside world acknowledges his inability to perceive the reason for her fascination with the glass collection and expresses his misgivings about having to handle the little animals. His statement 'I'm pretty clumsy with things' (p.101), introducing as it does the long scene in which Jim starts probing into Laura's intimate being, is full of ominous forebodings. The only strategy Jim can think of to draw Laura away from her morbid fascination is to invite her to 'cut the rug a little' (p.102) to the waltz music coming from the Paradise Dance Hall. Jim thus lures Laura out of her dream-like universe and invites her to move with him into the world of the alley, to become identified with the innumerable couples moving indistinctly in the flickering light of 'deceptive rainbows' or seeking the relative privacy of the alleyway in search of a fleeting moment of intimacy.

As Jim swings Laura into motion they hit the little table. The unicorn falls to the floor, its horn broken off. In the course of the play the unicorn has come to stand for at least two things: for Laura herself and for the possibility of her escape into an unreal world of glass. The unicorn breaks, then—aptly, it would seem—at the moment when Laura emerges from the world of her lifeless companions and transfers the function of refuge to the person of Jim. The breaking of the unicorn marks the turning point in Laura's life. The flickering, unreal world of glass toys no longer suffices as she feels rising in her a desire to disregard her freakishness, to dance like all the others, to belong to the real world.

The event symbolises a kind of emotional deflowering, an irreversible loss of childlike innocence, the unavoidable mutilation that Williams sees as necessarily accompanying the process of growing up. Laura's reaction to the accident, however, reveals that she is less concerned about what she has lost than about what she vaguely senses might be a gain: 'It doesn't matter. Maybe it's a blessing in disguise . . . It's no tragedy, Freckles. Glass breaks so easily—no matter how careful you are—the traffic jars the shelves and things fall off them . . . Now he will feel more at home with the other horses, the ones that don't have horns' (p.104). Her surprisingly mild comment brings to the surface her deep-seated desire to 'feel more at home with the others'. Excited at the prospect of being able to identify with the patrons of the Paradise Dance Hall—she is 'laughing breathlessly' (p.103) a moment before the incident—Laura does not reproach Jim with clumsiness but instead indirectly expresses her gratitude to him for his part in ending an era.

Her expression of gratitude is qualified, however, by the fact that she equates Jim's effect on the unicorn with that of the heavy traffic outside. Jim, then, is obliquely identified with the hubbub outside, with destructive trucks and lorries. In this speech of Laura's, Williams masterfully manages to maintain the ambiguous value of Jim at this crucial moment in the girl's life: a potential saviour on the one hand, he is also her possible destroyer. Now that he has charmed her away from her lifeless friends, Jim the parlour psychiatrist imagines a shortcut that would miraculously make Laura come fully alive: 'Somebody needs to build your confidence up and make you proud instead of shy and turning away and—blushing—Somebody—ought to—Ought to—*kiss* you, Laura!' (p.106).

The new breath Jim wants to inspire in Laura is, in his opinion, what will make her capable of living in his world. However, the warning of Laura about her favourite glass animal—'Oh, be careful—if you breathe, it breaks!' still reverberates in the air as Jim draws Laura to him and 'kisses her on the lips'. The revelation of the world of physical intimacy unleashes in Laura a store of hidden feelings whose intensity is conveyed through her changing expression and prolonged silence. As he releases her, 'she sinks on the sofa with a bright, dazed look'; after a moment, when he addresses her, 'she looks up, smiling, not hearing the question' (p.106). As he offers her a piece of candy 'she doesn't seem to hear him but her look grows brighter even' (p.107). Only as Jim proceeds with his revelation about the existence of a fiancée, rhapsodising insensitively about 'the power of love' (p.108), does Laura's blissful look disappear. As the cruel fact dawns upon her that after taking her away from her enchanted sphere, Jim cannot take her any further, Laura is literally thrown off balance by the violent contrast between her expectations and this experience, as successive stage directions make clear: 'Laura sways slightly forward and grips the arm of the sofa . . . Leaning stiffly forward, clutching the arm of the sofa, Laura struggles visibly with her storm' (p.108).

By the end of Jim's speech, the illumination of his passage in Laura's life is completely gone: 'The holy candles in the altar of Laura's face have been snuffed out. There is a look of almost infinite desolation' (p.108). After a pause of crushing despair, Laura 'opens her hand again on the broken glass ornament. Then she gently takes his hand and raises it level with her own. She carefully places the unicorn in the palm of his hand, then pushes his fingers closed upon it'. What Jim takes with him is the symbol of Laura's short-lived hopes, a souvenir of the normal feelings he aroused in her for too brief a moment. Giving up the broken unicorn, Laura symbolically gives up all hope of ever being an average girl, all desire of ever realising in the outside world the deeper yearnings Jim has aroused in her.

Immediately after surrendering the mutilated glass figurine, Laura retreats to the only refuge still available: 'She rises unsteadily and crouches beside the victrola to wind it up' (p.109). This slight motion underlines Laura's renunciation of the world, making it clear, as Nelson has noted, that 'She will never allow a Jim O'Connor to happen to her again.' A few moments later, when the news of Jim's engagement reaches Amanda, the cameo tragedy of the broken unicorn acquires the larger overtones of a social catastrophe. In Amanda's eyes Jim was, we should remember, the fairy-tale prince who was to put the glass slipper on Laura's foot and make the American Dream come true. His defection prevents Amanda from glossing over the ugly facts any longer: 'The effort, the preparations, all the expense! The new floor lamp, the rug, the clothes for Laura! All for what? To entertain some other girl's fiance! Go to the movies, go! Don't think about us, a mother deserted, an unmarried sister who's crippled and has no job!' (pp.113-4).

The pathos of the situation is enhanced by Amanda's use of words she has hitherto banned not only from her own vocabulary but from Tom's. Her lapse reveals that with the gentleman caller's departure, the dreams and illusions which the spectator had been tempted to share with her, have collapsed. Her last speech leaves the audience and the reader, who know from Tom's conversation with Jim that Tom is about to follow in his father's footsteps, with even less hope than Amanda. The final pantomime, presenting her consoling gestures towards Laura as an endlessly repeated dumbshow, emphasises the profound despair of the play's bleak vision.

The set

The Glass Menagerie is set in St Louis, the principal city of Missouri, a town Tennessee Williams knew well from having spent several childhood years there. The picture of urban life presented in the play bears clear traces of the personal aversion to big city existence Williams conceived when he was forced as an eight-year-old to leave the rural community of Clarksdale, Mississippi, where his grandfather was an Episcopalian minister, to live in St Louis, where his father had been promoted to a managerial position.

'Neither my sister nor I could adjust ourselves to life in a mid-western city . . . in a perpetually dim little apartment in a wilderness of identical brick and concrete structures with no grass and no trees . . . only ugly rows of apartment buildings the colour of dried blood and mustard.'* Although the playwright acknowledged that 'the apartment where we lived wasn't as dingy and poverty-stricken as that in the play',** the set attests to his horrified reaction to the shabbiness of his new surroundings.

'The Wingfield apartment is in the rear of the building, one of those vast hivelike conglomerations of cellular living-units that . . . are symptomatic of the impulse of this largest and fundamentally enslaved section of American society to avoid fluidity and differentiation and to exist and function as one interfused mass of automatism' (p.21). The repellent uniformity of the habitat, explicitly presented by Williams as an architectural extension of the lower-middle-class tendency to social conformity, represents self-imposed imprisonment, the voluntary abdication of personal uniqueness. As a poet—in Williams's view someone endowed with heightened sensitivity and awareness of individual differences—Tom is painfully aware of the squalid sameness of his surroundings, which becomes one of the things prodding him to escape.

The Wingfield apartment overlooks an alley. It is flanked on both sides by other 'dark, narrow alleys which run into murky canyons of tangled clothes-lines, garbage cans, and the sinister lattice-work of neighbouring fire escapes' (p.21). Although these dead-end streets, like the drab rows of apartments, remain unseen by the playgoer, they acquire immediate reality and a definite symbolic meaning for the reader. They make it clear that Tom's final departure in a burst of anger is not an act of deliberate cruelty but rather the desperate act of a man who fears being entombed alive.

Visible on the side of the stage are the landing and first steps of a fire escape which is, unexpectedly, the only means of getting in and out of the apartment, a feature meant to emphasise its prisonlike nature. Even if, at the end of the play, it turns into Tom's route of escape from his unbearable situation, its overtones of liberation are strongly qualified. The fire escape leads Tom away from 'the implacable fires of human desperation' into an existence of aimless wandering and perhaps an involuntary military career in the Second World War.

The interior of the apartment occupied by the Wingfields is revealed, at the end of Tom's opening commentary, through the grim rear wall of the building. It is composed essentially of a living room (downstage), 'which also serves as a sleeping-room for Laura, the sofa unfolding to

---

*Williams, Tennessee: 'Facts About Me', record cover, *Tennessee Williams Reading from His Works*, Caedmon TC 1005, 1952.
**Quoted in Van Gelder, Robert: 'Playwright with a good conceit', *The New York Times*, 22 April 1945.

make her bed' (p.21), and, on the other side of a second proscenium arch, a dining room (upstage). The dim lighting throughout the play, the dusty curtains and the shabby-genteel furniture reinforce the overtones of poverty in this middle-city prison.

The set so far described might well fit a naturalistic drama. However, Williams was aiming at something quite different, for 'The scene is memory and is therefore nonrealistic. Memory takes a lot of poetic licence. It omits some details; others are exaggerated, according to the emotional value of the articles it touches, for memory is seated predominantly in the heart' (p.21). Clearly the author intended not realism in this set, but atmosphere. This view is restated, together with Williams's conception of symbolism and 'plastic theatre', in the Production Notes to the play.

The unhappiest of the devices used by Williams in *The Glass Menagerie* to create his 'plastic theatre' was a screen on which images or titles were to be projected—an idea obviously borrowed from the 'epic' forms of Erwin Piscator* and Bertolt Brecht,** which Williams had discovered during his studies at the New School for Social Research, at the time also the academic home of Piscator. The device was intended to help the audience's understanding by 'strengthen[ing] the effect of what is merely allusion in the writing and allow[ing] the primary point to be made more simply and lightly than if the entire responsibility were on the spoken lines' (p.8). Unlike Brecht, who uses the same device to project political or social comments, Williams would have liked, had his producers concurred with his plan, to fill the screen with pictures or slogans that could 'have a definite emotional appeal' (p.8) for the spectators. Thus he wanted the words 'où sont les neiges?'† to be projected during Amanda's nostalgic recollections of Blue Mountain; another phrase, 'the crust of humility', would have appeared in the background on the occasion of her discouraged sermon to Laura after the business college failure.

*Erwin Piscator (1893–1966) was a theatrical director famous for the ingeniousness of his staging techniques. An outspoken sympathiser with the working-class, he used his 'total theatre' innovations—films, newsreels, optical and acoustic effects—for leftist political aims. He remained in the United States from 1939 to 1951.

**Bertolt Brecht (1898–1956) is the most outstanding German playwright of the first half of the twentieth century. His theories about epic theatre, influenced by Piscator, led to the development of new acting methods and stage practices such as the famous 'alienation effect', the use of masks, the introduction of songs and slogans and screen projections, interrupting the action of plays with social or moral comments. Brecht's aim was to prevent the traditional identification of spectator and hero: instead, he wanted the audience to remain critically aloof in order better to pass judgement on the characters and the action.

†From the refrain question 'mais où sont les neiges d'antan?' (but where are the snows of yesteryear?) in 'La Ballade des Dames du Temps Jadis' by the French poet François Villon (1431–?63).

In other, less obvious cases, the legends would appear unintentionally ludicrous and would introduce a dismaying note of parody into the most poignant scenes. For example, when Laura is trying to overcome her paralysing shyness and come to dinner with the gentleman caller, Williams wanted the legend to read 'terror'. Then, as she stumbles toward the dining-room table, with Amanda and Tom rushing to her rescue, the screen was to comment 'ah'. Finally, when Jim O'Connor confesses that he is already engaged, destroying Amanda's dreams, the words projected were to have been 'the sky falls'. Fortunately, Eddie Dowling, the first director of the play, sensed how damaging the projections might prove in a play as delicate as *The Glass Menagerie*, and ordered them out. Williams did not dispute the decision and admitted that 'the extraordinary power of Miss Taylor's performance made it suitable to have the utmost simplicity in the physical production' (p.8). He never later insisted that the device be reintroduced on stage, although he included it in the published manuscript.

More felicitous than the intrusive device of the screen was the use of a musical motif composed by Paul Bowles and called 'The Glass Menagerie'. It is like 'circus music, not when you are on the grounds or in the immediate vicinity of the parade, but when you are at some distance and very likely thinking of something else. It seems under those circumstances to continue almost interminably and it weaves in and out of your preoccupied consciousness; then it is the lightest, most delicate music in the world and perhaps the saddest. It expresses the surface vivacity of life with the underlying strain of immutable and inexpressible sorrow' (p.9). The melody, connected with the figure of the narrator, contributes to the impression that the events of the play are remote in time, perceived as a memory-misted song that lingers hauntingly in his mind: 'It serves as a thread of connection and allusion between the narrator with his separate point in time and space and the subject of his story' (p.9). A background obligato, it weaves the various episodes together, restating in musical terms at the opening and closing of almost every scene the nostalgia that suffuses the narrator's recollections of Laura's fragile beauty.

The final extra-literary device on which Williams relies in this play is lighting, which he uses to emphasise emotional content. 'In keeping with the atmosphere of memory' (p.9), the stage is dim throughout the play. The Production Notes also, however, call for 'shafts of light . . . focused on selected areas or actors, sometimes in contradistinction to what is the apparent centre' (p.9). In the instance of Tom and Amanda's quarrel, in which Laura is a stunned onlooker, the spotlight is on her figure. Later, at supper, Laura's silently suffering figure on the sofa is again singled out as the visual centre.

Besides isolating the pathetic figure of Laura for emotional emphasis, the light should moreover tinge her suffering with overtones of purity and sanctity. It should have a quality distinct from the lighting used for characters, 'a peculiar pristine clarity such as light used in early religious portraits of female saints or madonnas' (p.10). Quality, intensity, and frequency of light should, then, together with the special melody, reveal not the 'banality of surfaces', as Eugene O'Neill called it, but the reality of the protagonists' inner selves. Light and music help achieve the aim ascribed by Williams, following O'Neill, to all such 'unconventional techniques': 'to find a closer approach, a more penetrating and vivid expression of things as they are' (p.7).

Is *The Glass Menagerie* a tragedy?

Critics have often used the word 'tragic' to describe the characters and the events of the play. The above question is therefore legitimate, but the answer cannot be clear-cut or definitive. Much here depends on the reader's conception of tragedy, on the definition he applies, and on his evaluation of the play in comparison with tragedies of the past or with contemporary 'tragic' works. Although the arguments vary from one evaluation to the next, the critical consensus at this point seems to be that *The Glass Menagerie* falls short of tragedy. We should not try to come up with a final answer, but in discussion of the problem the following points should be heeded.

It is generally felt that the characters in the play lack the stature of the older tragic heroes, that their values and their aims in life are not as exalted. Some critics express this succinctly by saying that the characters are not 'big' enough. This does not imply that they are not real or that their troubles are unimportant: all four may be experienced as intensely genuine characters, and the shattering of their lives has a great impact on an audience. But they are all failures, personal or social, in their own eyes or in the eyes of others, and as the drama unfolds they experience further failure. As one critic has put it, 'in the course of their drama they all perish a little'.*

Even more damaging to the play's claim to tragic status, the characters all appear to be doomed to fail from the very start. Whatever they do, however valiantly they struggle, however ingenious their strategies, they are never given a real chance; they are never in a position to right things. They appear from the outset as victims of 'circumstance, lost in a world beyond their comprehension—notice Amanda's observation that we live in such a mysterious universe' (p.86)—and overpowered by a situation which they have not created and which they cannot control. Their flight, then, is a desperate fending off of the inevitable, more often

---

*Nelson, Benjamin: *Tennessee Williams: The Man and his Work*, Ivan Obolensky, New York, 1961, p.109.

than not a retreat before an ineluctable fate. Tom's sailor attire in the Prologue clearly foreshadows the end of the play, reinforcing the sense of immediate doom that makes the destinies of the Wingfields pathetic and pitiable, but not tragic.

For tragic greatness rests in part on the ability of the exceptional individual to control or direct his destiny; tragedy further postulates essential awareness and conscious choices. The characters of *The Glass Menagerie* are denied these qualities from the very beginning, labelled as they are as members of 'the huge middle class of America . . . matriculating in a school for the blind . . . having their fingers pressed forcibly down on the fiery Braille alphabet of a dissolving economy' (p.2). For all its surface agitation, their existence is best described as 'passing . . . without any change or adventure' (p.30).

When all is said, Amanda, Laura, and Tom are weak, nervous, and self-conscious characters living outside reality in a world of illusion and make-believe (and we have shown that much the same could be argued about Jim). They are, to use Williams's later words, all guinea pigs in the laboratory of God—the playthings of an all-powerful being who is intent on vexing or destroying them. The universe of the play is completely determined biologically, psychologically, and socially; there is no room for free will.

The end of the play, too, lacks tragic grandeur. It offers no solution, no direction, no message. Neither death nor the courageous facing up to a harder life enhance the stature of the characters; all they manage to do is endure, to live out a fate they cannot alter. The world of *The Glass Menagerie* disappears in 'everlasting darkness', disposed of by a scenic trick, blown out 'not with a bang but a whimper'. It is a world of unalleviated gloom, not of tragic exaltation.

Religious symbolism

Numerous unobtrusive references to the Bible and Christian religious practice are scattered throughout the play. In his thorough analysis of this aspect of the play, Stein* points out that such references are associated with all four characters. Thus Amanda refers to 'Christian martyrs' (pp.38, 55) in both of her telephone conversations and to 'Christian adults' (p.52) in her conversation with Tom about instinct. In her few moments of silent suffering in Scene Four, before Tom apologises, the music is the 'Ave Maria' (p.48), the musical composition to which the words of the Angel to Mary in the Annunciation episode are tradition-

*Stein, Roger B.: '*The Glass Menagerie* Revisited: Catastrophe without Violence', *Western Humanities Review* 18 (Spring 1964), pp.141–53; reprinted in Stephen S. Stanton (ed.): *Tennessee Williams: A Collection of Critical Essays*, Prentice-Hall, Englewood Cliffs, New Jersey, 1977, pp.36–44.

ally set. 'Annunciation' (p.56) is in fact the word that was to appear projected on the screen at the beginning of Scene Five. Early in the play, Laura says that the suffering look on her mother's face reminds her of 'the picture of Jesus' mother in the museum' (p.33).

The Christian references that cluster around Tom appear primarily, although not exclusively, in his account of the magic act. Malvolio, the magician, may even be considered a caricature of Christ. On his music-hall stage he turned water into wine, as Christ did at the Cana wedding; the rainbow-coloured scarf ironically recalls the biblical sign of God's reconciliation with man after the flood; and the 'wonderfullest trick of all', in which he escapes from a nailed coffin, is a grotesque distortion of the events of Easter, an allusion reinforced by Amanda's refrain of 'Rise and Shine'.

It is around Jim O'Connor, however, that most of the religious symbolism is centred. It is through him that the Christian allusions acquire their keenest meaning. Jim is first introduced through his picture in *The Torch*, a title which immediately associates him with light. Later, on hearing his full name, Amanda exclaims 'That, of course, means fish', a comment which, 'functions not only literally, since Jim is Irish Catholic, but also figuratively, for fish is the traditional symbol of Christ'. For those attentive to the Christian symbolism used by the author, Jim might become identified with Christ, a saviour-figure. The air of expectancy created by the circumstances of the play is reinforced by Tom's description of the family's guest as a Messiah figure: 'he is the long-delayed but always expected something that we live for' (p.23).

Jim's arrival is accompanied by rain (p.74), underlining the hopes of fertility and renewal connected with his visit. Those overtones are, however, soon contradicted by Laura's unsuccessful attempt to come to the table and the ironic effect, in view of the outcome of the play, of Tom's grace: 'For these and all thy mercies—God's Holy Name be praised' (p.84). Even before the essential scene between Laura and Jim, an incident with symbolic significance strongly qualifies the hopes aroused by the gentleman caller's visit. The failure of the electricity supply after dinner, perhaps a glance ahead to the blackouts that are to come with the Second World War, prompts Amanda's joking question, 'Where was Moses when the lights went out?' (p.85). She thus evokes the figure of another saviour, whose fate it was to bring his flock only to within sight of the Promised Land. The suggestion of failure is reinforced by Amanda's answer to her own question: 'In the dark!' (p.85). Jim's potential as modern saviour is thus indirectly stated even as Williams obliquely hints at the elements that make his success doubtful. The after-dinner scene confirms the ominous forebodings: Jim is an abysmal failure in the role.

For Laura he institutes a modern mock-communion. At the outset of the scene he offers her dandelion 'wine' (p.89), which she shares with him; later, he completes the sacrament, as he is about to tell her the cruel truth, by presenting her with the ironically named 'Life Savers' (p.107), which she has no time to accept. The 'ceremony', moreover, is interspersed with Jim's accompanying advice to Laura, a commentary that Stein has aptly described as 'a Dale Carnegie* version of the Sermon on the Mount—self-help rather than divine help'. The whole scene is delicately suffused with the trembling light of a candelabrum rescued from a defunct Southern church, emphasising the religious overtones.

At the very centre of the final scene and of the Christian symbolism of the play is the unicorn incident. The unicorn is a traditional Christian symbol, usually representing purity. A frequent subject of Christian iconography, it is often represented as the leader of the pure animals and opponent of the serpent, leader of the impure animals. Early Christians even equated the unicorn with Christ himself. In the light of this traditional symbolism, Jim's instrumental role in the disfigurement of the unicorn is the final, decisive denial of his role as Messiah. What he ultimately takes with him is as much an emblem of his identity as a broken, powerless saviour as a souvenir of Laura.

For Laura, the unicorn breaks, appropriately enough, at a moment when the tinsel Paradise across the alley is haloed with an illusory light of salvation (the deceptive rainbow?). When this fades away with Jim's hasty departure, Laura is left with a dark emptiness. Far from being Laura's saviour, Jim destroys the one emblem of the saviour in her existence, leaving her in the dark. The blackout at the end of the play underlines the thoroughly pessimistic outcome.

By virtue of the religious overtones surrounding him, Jim is tentatively cast as a potential redeemer. The redemptive process is interrupted before its completion and the very discontinuity conveys the author's derisive attitude towards man's perennial but futile hope for some kind of salvation from a world and a condition in which he is trapped. It also vividly illustrates Williams's debunking of the religious tradition that fostered this illusion in the West and is now, after two thousand years of preaching, rejected or reduced to forms and formulas, mechanical gestures and empty words that have lost whatever original vitality they may have had and are totally unable to alleviate modern man's predicament. As Stein concluded: 'The bleakness of Williams' vision in *The Glass Menagerie* is complete.'

---

*Dale Carnegie (1888-1955) was a famous American teacher of public speaking. His book *How to Win Friends and Influence People* (1936) had a world-wide success. In it he elaborated methods of developing poise, concentration and self-confidence.

Part 4

Hints for study

THE FOLLOWING SPECIMEN questions and answers suggest problems that have been debated by the critics: they also draw attention to passages or techniques not analysed in detail thus far, although some have been brought up already and partially discussed in the comments on individual scenes. Building on his thorough knowledge of the play and on these Notes, the student should be able to organise his own thoughts on these various topics before turning to the proposed solutions. These Notes should at any rate be tested against the student's understanding of the text and, when possible, his acquaintance with the play in performance. They should be considered neither definitive nor exhaustive.

---

1. Consider the criticism that *The Glass Menagerie* is a 'sentimental' play.

In order to organise his response to this crucial question, the student should keep the following in mind: (1) the autobiographical nature of the material; (2) the narrator's remarks on memory in his first speech (p.23); (3) the author's description of the various characters; (4) the effect of many passages in performance (the student should read the play aloud, distributing the roles to different participants, and should carefully note those passages that could be said to contain comical or ironical elements); (5) the possible effect in this context of the device of the narrator and the use of images and words projected on a screen.

When a play is described as 'sentimental' the comment is usually derogatory: it suggests that somehow the feelings expressed are excessive or inappropriate, that the author indulges his taste for emotion or sadness. Yet in a play that is frankly presented as 'memory' one expects to find—indeed is ready to accept—a great degree of sentiment, because memory often softens the past and even unpleasant events are transformed by the warm glow of recollection. As narrator, Tom tells us that 'The play is memory. Being a memory play, it is dimly lighted, it is sentimental, it is not realistic. In memory everything seems to happen to music. That explains the fiddle in the wings.' The unabashedly sentimental quality of the writing is thus made acceptable by the very nature of the memory play, yet Williams is well aware of the danger of self-indulgence and tawdriness. He never lets his evident sympathy for the characters interfere with his objectivity. He sees his creations with compassion, understanding, and even admiration, as in the case of Amanda. But he does not blind himself to their obvious shortcomings, their grotesque mannerisms, or their naïve idealism.

While Amanda may be a paragon of 'endurance', justly described as 'heroic', she is at the same time and in equal measure a social snob, a vain former belle, and, in her ambitions for Laura, a cruelly insensitive blunderer. But often in performance she appears unwittingly comical. Her appearance in bathrobe and metal curlers in Scene Three; Tom's sarcastic comments at her expense in Scene One, 'I bet you could talk', and 'What did he leave his widow?'; the long 'Annunciation' in which Tom teasingly withholds information from her in Scene Five; or her own silly excitement in Scene Six over her actual meeting with Jim, all provoke laughter. Each time, the potential for sentimentality contained in her is deflated: emotion and sentiment are controlled by humour and wit.

Similarly, in presenting Jim, the playwright has introduced many ironical elements (see Part 3, 'Characters') that prevent us from taking him at face value when he describes his plans for the future or his visions of American democracy. In the long tender scene with Laura, the naïveté of Jim's apprentice psychologist's jargon, the simplistic nature of his remedies, not to mention his furtive glances at himself in the mirror, his chewing gum, and the awkwardness of his departure, all confirm his simple nature while at the same time emphasising the comic aspect of it. Again the author's clear-sighted, wry humour keeps the emotions in check.

From a more technical point of view, the use of a narrator as a frame which firmly sets the events of the play in the past serves as another controlling device. The audience, and to an even greater extent the readers, remain at one remove from the drama and are thus less tempted to identify with the characters or to share their sentimental outbursts. Things reported have less emotional impact than things immediately witnessed.

Had the screen been used (and it has in recent productions) it would have constituted yet another means of counterbalancing the potential sentimentality of the play. Brecht and Piscator, from whom Williams presumably borrowed the idea, meant the projected captions and pictures to provoke the spectators into realising that, far from experiencing real life, they were in fact watching a performance given by actors on a stage. Although Williams seems to have thought that his screen could have 'definite emotional appeal', it is difficult to believe that legends such as 'terror!' or 'ah'—to take only two examples—would not have an alienating effect in the scene in which Laura, terrified by the arrival of Jim, falls as she stumbles towards the supper table. On balance, then, if it cannot be denied that the very nature of the play is sentimental in the sense that it involves an emotional recollection of painful events; neither can it be overlooked that the play contains a number of subtly interwoven touches of humour or irony which the director and his actors can use to prevent the basic emotional truth of the play from deteriorating into sentimentality.

2. Consider the criticism that *The Glass Menagerie* is a clever juxtaposition of scenes rather than a unified play.

You should be able to organise your discussion as above, taking into account what has been said about the structure of the play, its chronological development, its static nature, its character as 'memory', unifying elements mentioned in the analysis of the set, and the comments on the concomitant motifs of the father and the gentleman caller.

3. Re-read the two telephone conversations of Amanda and the comments and questions contained in the discussion of Scene Three. Determine (i) the structural function of the telephone conversations; (ii) their characterising function; and (iii) the ironic overtones introduced by the detailed information given about the magazine.

The two 'arias' appear respectively at the start of Scene Three and at the end of Scene Four, thus framing, critics have observed, scenes of the quarrel and reconciliation in terms of the deflection and then resumption of Amanda's pleas. As mentioned in the comments on Scene Three, the phone conversations constitute clear indications of the practical side of Amanda's character. They help to show that while sometimes she may be a silly dreamer, there is, as Tichler* has remarked, 'an anomalous element of practicality encased in her romantic girlishness'. This dichotomy or internal tension is the essence of her character.

Besides suggesting the financial struggles brought on by the Depression, both episodes, then, dramatise Amanda's courage and stamina. And both introduce trenchant irony. The very title of the magazine Amanda tries to sell, *The Homemaker's Companion*, is in ironic contrast with the fact of her marital failure and her admission that she is 'not at all [domestic]. I never was a bit' (p.80). Heightening this irony is the fact that Amanda's 'homemaker's' money is destined first to finance Laura's disaster in business school, and second, when the business school scheme proves unworkable, to help 'feather out the nest' to lay the trap for the gentleman caller—both projects that in the end reveal Laura's shortcomings in the domain of 'homemaking'.

In contrast to Tom, who calls his mother's periodical 'a magazine for matrons' and describes its contents contemptuously, Amanda praises

*Nancy Tischler, *op. cit.*, p.97.

the author Bessie Mae Hopper's romanticised view of reality, in which the 'horsey set on Long Island' is a Northern version of her own Blue Mountain fantasies. Her anticipation of a success for Bessie Mae Hopper's effort comparable to that of *Gone With the Wind* (p.38) gives her escapism even broader implications. The allusion to Margaret Mitchell's best-seller of the Depression years ranks Amanda with most of her fellow Americans, who sought in it an imaginative escape from their disheartening surroundings. Amanda's literary references thus acquire a larger social significance.

Equally revealing, but restricted to Amanda's own personal fantasies, is her comment on the lady author's previous contribution to *The Homemaker's Companion*: 'It's by Bessie Mae Hopper, the first thing she's written since *Honeymoon for Three*. Wasn't that a strange and interesting story?' (p.55). Here again both the title of the serial and Amanda's praise reveal the ultimate aim of the magazine campaign, the seduction of a gentleman caller, who will then marry Laura and turn the wishful thinking of the title into reality. The striking contradiction in the title itself, however, underlined by Amanda's appreciation of the 'strangeness' of the story, suggests once again the impractical, impossible character of Amanda's project. The two magazine 'arias', although disclosing the realistic component of Amanda's nature that prompts her to take practical steps in dealing with reality, are thus equally revealing of her tendency to glance backward, her retreat into memories of the past.

---

4. Re-read the stage directions in Scene Two describing Amanda's physical appearance and particularly her clothes and pocketbook. The description is one of the most detailed in the whole play. Basing your analysis on what you know so far of Williams's use of clothing for expressive purposes (see the comments on Scenes Two, Three, and Four), determine the function of Amanda's costume and accessories in this particular instance.

Amanda's appearance when she returns from the visit to the business college, decked out in her Sunday best for the D.A.R. meeting she did not attend, constitutes a symbol of her entire situation. The cheap coat with its imitation fur collar, unsuited for the winter season; the old-fashioned hat; the general shabbiness of her entire appearance, attest to the straitened financial circumstances of the family and provide a vivid contrast to Amanda's golden youth.

These overtones are reinforced through her clutching of an 'enormous black patent-leather pocketbook with nickel clasps and initials' and by her 'hopeless fingering of the huge pocketbook' later in the scene.

It is appropriate that this reminder of her past wealth—suggested by the size of the property and its clasps and initials—should be constantly present while she discusses the collapse of her 'plans and provisions' for the future. Her 'clasping' and 'hopeless fingering' reveal the basic financial insecurity for which she is trying to compensate. The presence of the pocketbook throughout the conversation indicates that in this scene between mother and daughter, Laura's emotions are of little consequence to Amanda. The marriage plans which she is about to broach are thus introduced primarily as an economic device, a way out of the family's penuriousness. The patent-leather pocketbook is here the visual correlative of Amanda's preoccupation.

---

5. Williams originally entitled his play *The Gentleman Caller*. The short story on which it is based is called *Portrait of a Girl in Glass*. Analyse the relevance of these titles; compare them to the final title, *The Glass Menagerie*.

Portrait of a Girl in Glass is a painfully literal presentation of the development of mental illness which led Rose, the playwright's sister, to an asylum at an early age. As indicated by the word 'portrait', the title of the short story, like the story itself, focuses on the pitiable figure of the heroine and introduces, through the reference to glass, hints of both fragile beauty and unnaturalness. It draws attention to the delicate loveliness of Laura but also to the strangeness that makes her unfit for life. Both overtones are felicitously preserved in the title of the play.

The film script of *The Gentleman Caller* is lost but the title itself suggests a shift in viewpoint. Although it seems to focus on a single character, the title in fact is an abstraction, suggesting less a person than what Tom in the play calls an 'archetype of the universal unconscious, the image of the gentleman caller' (p.37). That title, then, hints not at a person but at the obsession of the Wingfield household, not at a concrete being but at the futile hope the mother conceives, and at the refuge she unavailingly envisions for Laura. The final title recaptures these overtones as well.

The unexpected coupling in the final title of the words 'menagerie' and 'glass', of the idea of a zoo filled with living things and the image of clear, dead matter creates a strong semantic shock, similar to that communicated by the phrase 'girl in glass'. Here Williams joins with unusual flair the idea of visual beauty and vital inadequacy.

Following the movement from concrete to abstract already noticed in *The Gentleman Caller*, the title *The Glass Menagerie* moves away from any precise reference to a single character and focuses on the collection of glass objects which in the play constitutes, on its shelf in a corner, not only a privileged area isolated from the rest of the shabby surroundings but also a brittle, unreal world of escape. It evokes not only Laura's defence against reality but also that of all the characters in the play. It has been stressed that Amanda's 'plans and provisions' for Laura, Tom's dreams about the merchant navy, and Jim's starry visions of the future are all to some extent comparable to the easily shattered collection of figurines. The glass menagerie of the title does not epitomise the attributes of Laura alone—these are more precisely represented by the unicorn—but calls forth the beautiful and fragile dreams by which all the characters fend off reality.

Part 5
Suggestions for further reading

The text

The text used in these notes is that of The New Classics edition published by New Directions, New York, 1970. Reference is also made to the acting version published by Dramatists Play Service, New York, 1948. Students interested in the very fine process of revision that finally yielded the present text should compare it with the short story *Portrait of a Girl in Glass* (in *One Arm and Other Stories*, New Directions, New York, 1948). They are further referred to ROWLAND, JAMES L.: 'Tennessee's Two Amandas', *Research Studies* XXXV, 4, 1967, pp.331–40, which points out how even small changes may affect overall characterisation.

Biographical information

WILLIAMS, DAKIN and SHEPHERD MEAD: *Tennessee Williams: An Intimate Biography*, Arbor House, New York, 1983.

WILLIAMS, EDWINA DAKIN (as told to Lucy Freeman): *Remember Me to Tom*, Putnam, New York, 1963.

WILLIAMS, TENNESSEE: *Memoirs*, Doubleday and Company, New York, 1975.

Critical studies

JACKSON, ESTHER MERLE: *The Broken World of Tennessee Williams*, Wisconsin University Press, Madison and Milwaukee, 1965.

NELSON, BENJAMIN: *Tennessee Williams: The Man and His Work*, Ivan Obolensky, New York, 1961.

PARKER, R. B. (ED.): *The Glass Menagerie: A Collection of Critical Essays*, Prentice-Hall, Englewood Cliffs, New Jersey, 1983.

STANTON, STEPHEN S. (ED.): *Tennessee Williams: A Collection of Critical Essays*, Prentice-Hall, Englewood Cliffs, New Jersey, 1977.

THARPE, JAC (ED.): *Tennessee Williams: A Tribute*, University of Mississippi Press, Jackson, 1977.

TISCHLER, NANCY M.: *Tennessee Williams: Rebellious Puritan*, The Citadel Press, New York, 1965.

WEALES, GERALD C.: *Tennessee Williams* (University of Minnesota Pamphlets on American Writers), University of Minnesota Press, 1965.

Students interested in the development of the criticism devoted to Williams's work are referred to *The Tennessee Williams Newsletter* mentioned in the Introduction to this book (p. 8).

For further bibliographical information, the student should turn to:

GUNN, DREWEY WAYNE: *Tennessee Williams: A Bibliography*, The Scarecrow Press, Metuchen, New Jersey, 1980.

The author of these notes

GILBERT DEBUSSCHER teaches English and American Literature at the University of Brussels. He was educated at the University of Brussels and at the Yale School of Drama. He returned to Yale in 1980-1 under a joint Fulbright-ACLS Fellowship Program; from 1974 to 1980 he was president of the Belgian Luxembourg American Studies Association, and from 1975 to 1980 Secretary of the European Association for American Studies. He is a member of the playreading committee of the Belgian Théâtre National. He has written *Edward Albee: Tradition and Renewal* (1967) and has published articles and reviews on American and avant-garde drama in scholarly journals.